Speaking with Strangers

Mary Cantwell

Houghton Mifflin Company   *Boston · New York · 1998*

For information about permission to reproduce
selections from this book, write to Permissions,
Houghton Mifflin Company, 215 Park Avenue South,
New York, New York 10003.

Library of Congress Cataloging-in-Publication Data
Cantwell, Mary.
    Speaking with strangers / Mary Cantwell.
        p.   cm.
    Sequel to: Manhattan, when I was young.
    ISBN 0-395-82751-5
        1. Cantwell, Mary — Journeys. 2. Voyages and travels.
I. Title.
G465.C275   1998
910.4 — DC21   97-48292   CIP

Printed in the United States of America

QUM 10 9 8 7 6 5 4 3 2 1

Book design by Melodie Wertelet

For Amy Gross,
who is all and more than is
meant by the word "friend"

If one cannot close a book of memories on
the deathbed, any conclusion must be arbitrary.

— *Graham Greene*

Speaking with Strangers

Prologue

The tide was wrong, I think, and maybe that was why the tenders couldn't come in to the pier and take us out to what I believe was the old *Queen Elizabeth*. Or it may have been the *United States*. Maybe the ocean liner, which at that distance and at twilight recalled a resurrected *Titanic*, wasn't ready to take on the people who were boarding at Le Havre. Or it may have been Calais.

I am sorry to be so vague, especially because I am proud of my good memory, and many have remarked upon it, but all I can remember is sitting on my one suitcase (I travel light) and waiting for hours to get going. Anywhere.

Neither can I remember how I got to the pier, although obviously it was on the boat train from Paris. I can't remember what I ate, or what I was wearing, or if I spoke to anyone, or any landscape except vast fields of yellow mustard. What I do remember is the pier and the man sitting on the suitcase beside me. He, too, had only one, old and wrapped with rope, because otherwise it wouldn't have closed. He was old as well, and dressed with the kind of decency that proclaims that traveling is an event to be treated with solemnity, respect.

"Have you ever read the great Polish writer Joseph Conrad?" he asked me. I turned, startled. We had never even exchanged glances, and, besides, the pier, for all the hundreds waiting on it, was very quiet. We might as well have been waiting for Charon.

"Yes, I have," I answered, but in truth I had forgotten almost everything but the "fascination of the abomination." It was a tag line of mine, trotted out for any and all revolting occasions and lending me (I thought) a certain literary aura.

"I am from Poland," he said. "I have just come from there."

Then the story came out, in slow, thick English.

When the old man was twelve or so, his mother and father and a brother or two had emigrated to the United States — to Chicago, as I recall. What his life was there — his work, his family, his dailiness — I have no idea. But I did hear about how he had saved for years for this trip. He had planned to see the town in which he was born, of whose houses he still had faint images and along whose streets he was sure he could still find his way. But when he arrived at the place to which memory and an old map had taken him, there was no town, only a crossroad where it once had been. The war had erased it, and with it erased his origins. Joseph Conrad was his Poland now.

I am not sure how much Conrad he himself had read. He talked about the person, not his work, and not in detail. I doubt he knew any details. But he knew that Poland had produced a great writer, that it was his Poland that had produced the great writer, and as long as the great writer was talked about and read, his Poland still existed. The more he spoke of Conrad, the more I saw the crossroad turning into a town again, the houses taking shape, the streets emerging from the raw landscape.

Finally, the tenders arrived at the pier and we boarded,

but not together. In fact, I never saw him again. I was
traveling cabin; he was probably traveling third class. His
journey had not been a success. Even now, so many years
later, I can imagine him tracing maps, exercising his rusty
Polish, counting and recounting his money, riding springless
buses and cranky trains, only to arrive at nowhere.

Still, for those few hours on the dark pier, when we were
without landmarks, without anything but that distant, almost mythical ship to give us a sense of place, he managed,
because of "the great Polish writer Joseph Conrad," to put us
in his country. His country was built with words, and for a
little time, while we talked, he lived there. I wish I could say
I am happy about his momentary repossession of his roots,
but I know far too much about traveling back in time not to
discount the pain that is so often the aftermath of the journey. It must have been hard for him to have lost that town. It
must have been harder to have been wrenched from it again.

That was a long time ago, when my children were small and
my husband, about to be my former husband, was desperate
to replace me and I seized every chance I got to leave home.
I was lucky. I had a lot of chances, because I was working on
a fashion magazine and was handy when it came to writing
travel articles. There were other chances, too, not necessarily
involving travel articles but always involving work. I would
not have traveled without the work. I could not have borne
the loneliness. But work drove me out into foreign streets to
talk to people with whom I would have been much too shy
even to share a nod. Work took me to places — the Anatolian
plateau, for instance, and Siberia — to which I would not
have dreamed of going. Work drove me to restaurants and
airports and to hotels in which I was sometimes the only
guest. And all the time that I was making notes and asking

questions and taking pictures with my little Brownie Star-mite, I was promising God that if only He would get me out of this hellhole I was in — Tashkent was the worst — I would stay home and be a good mother and never again leave my children, my wonderful, beautiful, innocent, and abandoned children. But then the chance would come once more, and, a bag slung over my shoulder, off I would go to the airport, so swollen with excitement it seemed I would push out the sides of the cab. At takeoff I would press my feet against the plane's floor, urging it into flight. Once I got to wherever I was going, though, I was so stripped of the familiar that I was skinless and would promise God once again that if only He would get me out of this hellhole I was in, I would stay home and be a good mother and never again leave my children, my wonderful, beautiful, innocent, and abandoned children.

Eventually the day came when I didn't have to do it anymore; travel like that, I mean. I could stay home. I didn't have to sit with strangers anymore, talking about Joseph Conrad and creating a country whose only boundaries were words. Piety would have me say that it was my daughters who brought me back into the land of pots and pans and beds and pillows and homework that had to be checked and suppers that had to be cooked. The joy on their faces when they saw me making Sunday pancakes or unpacking grocer-ies while singing a song my younger had invented, a song that involved endless repetitions of "Oh, juicy spaghetti, oh, juicy spaghetti," put something bubbly, something like gin-ger ale, in my veins. But that day was long in coming, and during the five or so years in which I rolled about the world like a billiard ball looking for a pocket, watching my girls was often like looking at them through the wrong end of a telescope.

Even when the three of us were together in front of the television set, the two of them huddled against me like cuddling cats, they seemed far away. Everything and everyone was far away. In the office and on the street I had to wear dark glasses even when there was no sun, because crying had my eyes chronically swollen, and what I saw through those shaded lenses was almost always in miniature, too distant to seem real. It was only when I trailed my children to school in the morning (they wanted their classmates to think they were allowed to walk alone) that I saw them full size: one fair, one dark, their little rumps twitching under their pleated skirts and their knee socks starting the slow descent toward their shoes.

Now, when I look at old photographs of my daughters, I see the desolation on the face of the younger, sitting on her rocking horse and clutching our impossible dog, Fred, and am touched by the little ribbon the older used to tie around her throat in imitation of a choker. But then, except for those minutes during our carefully distanced walks to school, I might as well have been gazing from a star.

Often I was deaf as well. "Mom, Mom," my children would cry when I settled into silence, trying to pull me back into their world. But I didn't want to see, not really, or to hear or talk. I wanted to be with Papa, buried beside him in St. Mary's Cemetery in Bristol, Rhode Island, reunited with someone who was faithless only in dying. But I couldn't go, couldn't slide beneath the grass that covered him. Being a mother denied me death and made me resentful. Sometimes I would look at my girls, my beauties, and think, "If it weren't for you two, I could leave."

No. To return to my children and to sight and sound and speech, I had to go far away and become acquainted with the only companion I have ever been able to rely upon. As long as I had a pencil and paper and notes to make for my insignificant little articles, I was not alone. With work to do, I could exit a world in which I was restless and confused and, above all, haunted by people who are shards and ashes, if they are anything at all now, and enter one in which it seemed morphine was dripping on my soul. Here I was calm; here, although I was actually more awake than in any elsewhere, I could sleep.

One

The morning of the day my children and I left the house we had lived in with their father — the house with the bunny wallpaper in their bedroom and the wooden valet from Brooks Brothers in ours — to move farther west on Greenwich Village's Jane Street, I was sitting with a friend in its tiny backyard.

"Would you ladies please move your chairs forward?" one of the moving men called out. "I've got to do some work with this window."

Obedient, we moved our chairs out of the shade and into the sun. Behind us, only two or so feet from where we had been sitting, the air conditioner fell to the ground. Had we not been told to move, we would have been killed. Still, neither of us paled, neither of us scared up so much as a tremble. "It's an omen" was all my friend said. "You were *meant* to leave this place."

Some hours later, with the children at my family's home in Rhode Island and the house bare of all but my bed and a few cartons, I went to a cocktail party way uptown, grateful that someone from my office had thought to invite me on a night when I would otherwise have been walking through the empty rooms, crying, maybe, and feeling the strange pain that seemed to twist my ribs whenever I thought of my husband — my husband who was happy now and free of the marriage that I had ruined. "How did you ruin it?" friends would ask, but I could never answer. I just knew it, that was all, knew it just as surely as I once had known that to step on a crack was to break my mother's back. I did not believe in fate or happenstance, only in my power to destroy. "That tongue of yours . . . those hands of yours . . . that temper of yours will get you into trouble someday," I was told in childhood. My mother was right. I was a killer.

Some of the guests were friends, the rest were strangers, and one of the latter was drunk. In those days I was a pretty woman, but there was something about my face, something that seemed to condemn, I guess, that aroused hostility — and, at the same time, attraction — in those who had had one too many. This man was no different. While his wife stood by, smiling limply, he made a few rude remarks about my having arrived late, tried to goad me into responding to a couple of dirty jokes, and finally said, "Who stuck the stick up your ass?" Then he dared me to drink a full glass of Scotch. I took the dare. "You're dealing with an Irishman here," I said, trying for a tough sophistication that I had never possessed, had never had to possess.

When I was halfway through the Scotch, another man took the glass from my hand and told the drunk to cut it out. The wife kept smiling, the drunk moved off, and I left for what remained of my home, feeling as helpless as my mother did the first time she had to balance a checkbook. My father had died. He had always paid the bills, and when, not realizing that she had to figure in the ten cents for each check, she couldn't match the bank's tally with hers, she put her head down on the desk and cried the only tears I had seen her cry since his death. Now it was I who was unprotected. Without my husband, with whom I had spent my entire adult life, I had no defenses against drunks and their brutalities. I didn't even know how to come to a cocktail party unescorted. How could I know? In the past, when I had entered a party by myself, it was always with the knowledge that my husband was soon to appear, rushing in from the office and about to feel my proprietary hand on his arm.

I shall call him by his initial, B, because it is boring to repeat _husband_ again and again. Also, I have a bad habit, one that leads strangers to believe I am still married. In speaking of him, I always say "my husband," simply because he is the only one I have ever had. Besides, it is hard for me to believe that a piece of paper can end a marriage, any more than it can end a motherhood or a sisterhood. My mother is my mother, and that is that. My sister is my sister, and that is that. My husband was my husband, and he still is. True, I am unacquainted with that man who lives across town, that man who has gained a little weight, a little hearing aid, and — as they seem to me, in the few times I have seen him — capped teeth. But the boy who bought me books to improve my mind and a linen blouse and a cashmere sweater to improve my wardrobe when I was a junior in college: I am bound to him until my last breath.

"You're always lighting little candles to that guy," a man who once fancied himself a possible suitor said not long ago. Yes. They are to someone who occupies the same niche in my mind as the plaster saints before whom — the dime pushed in the slot, the flame fluttering — I knelt in childhood. Pray as I might, I never really believed in them. As time passes, I grow less and less able to believe in him. But I want to. If I go on lighting candles, it is because I cannot bear thinking that he was, in the end, only a figment of my imagination. To think that would be to do myself a kindness. But I have never been very kind to myself. I am my own Simon Legree.

During that childhood, in a town where the only official entertainments were the bowling alley and the movies, I spent every Friday night at a little stucco theater called the Pastime. When the movie — and the news and the serial and the short — was over, I was still not only at it but in it. Walking home, gripping my grandfather's hand, the elm trees soughing overhead and the salt air surrounding us, I was not Mary Lee Cantwell but Alice Faye or Betty Grable or Lana Turner. Thin, dark-haired, my teeth armored by braces, two elastic bands, and a plastic retainer, I even thought I looked like them. Years later, the elms and the salt air long behind me, I subwayed home alone to B from an evening at the Royal Ballet (it was Sadler's Wells then) and _Sleeping Beauty_, and tried to show him how a man named Brian Shaw danced the Bluebird Variation. My arms flapping, my leaps a mere six inches off our shag rug, I truly thought I was dancing. Once, leaving a Broadway show with B and an acquaintance who proclaimed himself "a truth-teller," I so persisted in unconscious mimicry of the heroine that the truth-teller told me to cut it out.

Retaining my edges was even more difficult when I was reading. Then, if the story was powerful enough, it erased my reality. The people I have been! Emma Bovary and Daisy Miller, of course. Lily Bart. Judith Hearne. I have been real people, too. Edith Thompson, who was hanged for killing her husband, and for whom I wept because her only crime was silliness. Madeleine Smith, who probably should have been hanged for killing her lover, but with whom I sympathized because he was a leech. And a woman, or several women, described in an article in _New York_ magazine.

The article was one of the magazine's usual 1970s ex-posés of the tragedies of urban life — life as a Puerto Rican pimp, for instance, or life as a black hooker. This time the tragedy of urban life had to do with the divorcées who, hair fresh from all-day rollers, buttocks molded by Lycra slacks, congregated at a roadhouse near the Long Island Expressway for five o'clock drinks with the men — married, most of them — who stopped there on the way home from work. I cried for those women. I was one of those women, not a magazine editor but a jobless housewife with teased hair and a pneumatic butt who cadged drinks, smokes, and feels from men in leisure suits. Leaving the party where that drunk had dared me to down a Scotch — how I had loved our cab rides home from parties, the New York streets glistening in the night and B solid beside me — I remembered that article. There it is, I said to myself, my fate.

My true fate, for a while anyway, was invisibility. A few weeks before my last day in the old house, a friend of B's had stopped me on the street and said solicitously. "Moving to a smaller place?"

"No," I snapped, "bigger," hating him for his curiosity and distrusting his concern. He and his wife, after all, had dispensed with me months before. So why the worried eyes, the voice dripping sincerity? I knew. Showing an interest in my future was akin to going to church once a year — Easter, say, or Christmas. The knees had been bent, the money dropped in the collection basket, the duty done.

But, then, everyone except my friends at the magazine had dispensed with me, and the world in which I had lived seemed imagined but not experienced. The seat I had occu-pied at dinner parties was still warm when my successor slid into it. If I wasn't surprised, it was because I had seen it happen so many times before, that curious disappearance into purdah that seemed so often the fate of first wives. It was as if we were all trial runs. Even our children were sometimes trial runs. "With my first two children, there was never time . . ." says the semifamous man to the newspaper interviewer, glorying in the issue from his aging loins. "But now I am discovering what it really means to be a father."

I might have missed that world more had we stayed in our old house. But our new house brought new vistas, new corners to turn. The first time we saw it (I was responding to an ad), my older daughter peeked around a closed shower curtain to see the tub. "So nosy!" I said, attempting to blush, but my embarrassment was faked. Had the present tenant not been there to show us around, I too would have peeked around the shower curtain. For I, like my eleven-year-old, was excited about unfamiliar faucets, foreign tiles. As time has proved, it is, above all else, what we have in common.

To remember life in our new house is to think of small blocks of color in a long gray ribbon. The blocks were the days and weeks when I woke up in countries in which, without a language to share with those along whose streets I walked, I was condemned to silence. I was condemned to envy, too, because those were their front doors they were opening and their groceries under their arms and their tables at which they would have their evening meal. Even so, I wallowed in the silence because it sharpened my senses. My ears were a fox's, my eyes an eagle's, and often I forgot I had any identity but that of traveler.

But I could not have survived without the long gray ribbon, the ordinary, to be deprived of which is my definition of hell. Still, on nights when I have run out of books, and all television palls, I sometimes bring out the colored blocks and play with them, freezing time, watching the woman I used to be in performance.

Soon after we moved in, I heard the leader of a Sunday-morning walking tour tell his charges that the house (Number 83, as it was known to the neighbors, who identified themselves by their addresses) was "Anglo-Italianate." But the neighbors, most of whom were standing about in what looked suspiciously like a receiving line the evening I emerged with the landlord after signing the lease, said it was a made-over stable. Whatever it was, it was built in 1856 and had an enormous mahogany bar in the cellar. "If worse comes to worst," said a friend who knew I was worried about the rent, "you can always open an afterhours club." Over the bar was inscribed: "On this site overlooking the majestic Hudson stood the William Bayard Mansion, where Alexander Hamilton, the first treasurer of the United States, died July 12, 1804, after his famous duel with Aaron Burr."

The rooms were tall and airy and painted my usual white, but it is the cellar I remember best: the bar and the tattered posters from rock concerts thumbtacked to dirty plaster walls and the cartons of 45s and rotting paperbacks left by the previous tenants. The landlord and his wife hoarded food. They came back from New Jersey supermarkets (no taxes) in what seemed a clown car, so crammed was it with staples and what they called "paper goods," then stored them in closets in the front. Once, curious, I opened one and saw what must have been fifty boxes of Social Tea Biscuits.

My old dishwasher was in that cellar, and an old wingchair, along with, in the back, the washer and dryer, around which crawled an army of shiny waterbugs. I was in that cellar constantly, hauling laundry and, bookish as always, quoting something appropriate from Yeats. Surely this, this unspeakable slum above which were rooms arranged as starkly and as beautifully (I thought) as a museum, was the foul rag-and-bone shop of my heart.

Because of a curious conjunction of streets, the block seemed cut off, isolated. Entering it, I always felt as if I were entering a stockade, a stockade that smelled strongly of the vanilla wafted through the open windows of the wholesale bakery at the corner. I liked that scent. I liked even better that, no matter how late I came home from work, some of the bakers would be sitting on the fire escape, taking a break from the ovens. Sometimes I'd wave at them, and sometimes they'd wave back. We were too distant and the sky too dark for us to recognize one another if we ever met by daylight. Still, on a street where little houses, their windows shrouded in curtains and blinds, turned blank faces to the world and the sidewalks emptied after eight, I thought them my compatriots, my _landsmen_.

In a town as old and settled as the place in which I was raised, one is known simultaneously by one's maiden name, one's husband's name, and, to some old-timers, by one's mother's maiden name. So it is not fatal to lose that second one. In fact, it is not fatal if you never acquire it, because identity also resides in your house, your street, your church, your great-grandfather's occupation. My grandmother had a cousin famous for her angel cakes, door prizes at many a church fair and the centerpieces of my every childhood birthday party. When she died, at a great age, there were enough people left to remember them, and therefore her, for the next twenty-five years. But in a city as provincial as New York, how are you identified except by your husband, your job, or your money? I loved my job, not so much for what I did at my desk but for what being at my desk did for me. It gave me a face, a voice, a manner. It gave me a personhood.

Even office friends, though, friends who'd been barely conscious of my having a husband, sometimes treated me as an amputee. "The one thing you musn't do," said the worldliest of them, a woman who herself had never married and had a long string of sexually uncertain escorts, "is give brave little dinner parties."

I didn't understand what she meant.

"*You* know," she continued. "You've always got to have a man at the foot of the table."

However, I didn't give dinner parties, brave or otherwise, although I liked to feed people, had memorized a book on carving, and could mix most drinks if they weren't too fancy. Raised with ritual, I held a wake instead. I did not think of myself as divorced but widowed, and when B called about the children or a check, the man I heard was a stranger. The voice was familiar — he had a beautiful voice, dark brown and as accentless as a radio announcer's — but I didn't know the speaker. I mourned the boy, I dreamed of him constantly, but I could not connect him with the man who had threatened custody suits and sanity hearings. Or I chose not to.

"Did I tell you about Shirley?" asked a woman whom I will call Rachel, herself recently separated from a husband who'd jumped everyone from assorted secretaries to their *au pair*, and eager to salve her miseries with those of the *salon des refusées* who seemed to constitute her friends. "Her exhusband used to make notes in book margins with a red ballpoint pen. Well, last week I borrowed a book from her, and guess what? She'd written in the margins with a red ballpoint pen! And did I tell you what she did the week before he divorced her in Mexico? He's a photographer and used that week to finish an assignment. And she, right behind him, drove all over the Southwest, staying in the motels he'd just left."

A few weeks later, Shirley telephoned me. "Rachel says we've had a similar experience, and I was wondering if you'd like to join me and some other women who've been through the same thing for lunch so we could talk about it."

I hung up as quickly as was decent. "No, it is not the *same thing*," I wanted to yell. "Nothing is the *same thing*. And, no, I don't want to talk about 'it.'"

It would have been like eating my vomit or leaving a corpse too long unburied. I had to inter my husband. Then, years later, I could resurrect him and make him a part of my past, to be discussed with the same nostalgia with which I discussed my former boyfriends and my former schoolteachers. I hadn't realized yet that a former husband, unless he'd been a cipher, will never slide into the same category.

So I held a wake, for myself as well as for him. Oh, my God, this reads grim; it wasn't grim. It just meant being an animal again; not even an animal, nothing quite so complex. Our new house had a garden in the back, and one summer morning when the sun was too bright on my book, I looked down toward the bluestone with which the garden was paved and saw an inchworm insinuating itself across a square. One of the children's cats tracked it with her nose, and the worm stopped and flattened itself into a still U. The cat lifted her nose and walked away, and the inchworm started moving again, right through the tiny space under the paw of another, sleeping cat. My style.

Cats. A dog. My younger daughter, the one I shall call Rose Red because her hair was black and her cheeks pink, loved pets, so at our previous house we'd had goldfish, a series of turtles, and an enormous snail who ceaselessly suckered his way along a big glass bowl. We had accidental pets too, small brown mice who could slide through hairline cracks. I grew adept at trapping them — the first time I disposed of a mouse, I felt I had achieved man's estate and was proud — but the children were appalled by my blood lust and could be appeased only by funerals. All the corpses got names. I remember only Mousie Brown Eyes.

Frustrated by the intractability of the furless (she had tried time after time to train her turtles to sit on the steps of their terraced plastic bowl), Rose Red languished for a dog and, tearless, stiff-backed, endured countless patch tests until declared only mildly allergic to animal fur. So we acquired Fred, a mongrel who looked like a Schnauzer on stilts and who, if left alone, avenged himself by toppling wastebaskets and chewing bed petticoats. Then Rose Red found "the most beautiful kitten in the world" at a block party and named her Eliza, and her sister, whom I shall call Snow White, because her hair was fair, appeared one day with Melanie, a half-grown tabby who'd been living in a vacant lot. When I objected, Snow White cried and said she wanted something of her own. So of course I said yes to this cat, who couldn't believe her luck and whose every meal was accompanied by furtive glances over her food bowl.

The calico up the street had kittens, one of which, its mother's clone, Rose Red acquired when it was weaned and which, after an evening with the dictionary looking up words that began with *cal*, she called Calypso.

So many pets were nuisances, especially the temperamental Fred, and Purina Cat Chow graveled the kitchen floor, but they gave life to a house in which the mother had none. I was keeping silence, playing dead, and if my daughters survived, it was because they were determined on all the little rituals — the bedtime stories, the Sunday breakfasts, the momentous trips to the supermarket — that made up the substance of their lives. But sometimes my children came home from school crying, because these were the days before every other mother was a single mother, and listening to what Mom and Dad had done over the weekend or hearing how the whole family was to gather for, say, Thanksgiving dinner was torture to them. My children did not want to be different from other children. My children were still young enough to want, desperately, to be like everybody else.

Some nights, though, I found myself unexpectedly happy because there was no body between me and the river-scented air that drifted through the open window. "I wonder if anyone will ever love me again," I would ask myself, but only because I thought I should. "You want to be like your mother, rocking on the porch all these years?" a cousin asked. I started to explain, then stopped, realizing suddenly that there was no longer an adult in the world to whom I owed an explanation for anything.

Except for my daughters, who invariably say, "You did the best you could," then laugh, there are still no adults to whom I owe an explanation. But I do indulge in description, because I like to tell stories. This, I am telling you, is what it was like to hold a wake for the living. It lasted, by my rough count, about six years, and much of it consisted — as do many wakes — of speaking with strangers.

There is a thing I have noticed about New Yorkers, many of them, anyway. Asked a direction, they will stretch a conversation that should have lasted one minute into three. If they are on a bus, they will stretch it even further. Perhaps it is because so many of them live alone. Words pile up behind their closed mouths like clothes that have been crammed into a too-small suitcase. Words were piling up behind my closed mouth, too, but because I was reluctant to utter them, I began to listen instead. I eavesdropped, although never on anyone I knew, resuming a habit of my childhood when, unnoticed in a corner of my grandmother's living room, I had listened to her and her friends speak of illness and death and wills, all of them growing more cheerful by the moment, so healthy was their interest in mortality and money.

Sitting on the bus, listening to people talk about their boyfriends or their jobs or the building super, who they were sure was in their apartments when they were out, was like reading novels whose endings one would never know. Did the girl who was going to Lincoln Center ever make up with Joe? Did the man who was worried about his company's sales ever get his raise? Was I accurate in believing that people who lived on the Upper West Side, by far the most vociferous of my fellow passengers, had the most tumultuous relationships with their landlords, supers, and block associations? I envied the people on the Upper West Side. Loneliness could not possibly be part of a life that involved so many phone calls, meetings, and rent strikes.

I began to listen to friends and acquaintances in a way I could not do when I was married. B and I had given dinner parties, many dinner parties, which were like tennis matches, but for the balls being _aperçus_ and the net, leg of lamb or _vitello tonnato_. The rallies were always long unless somebody, usually B, served an ace. Often there was no way to distinguish one voice from another — hardly surprising, since the guests, writers and editors for the most part, hewed on such occasions to the same intensely literary mode. Once I had made my own contributions to these tennis matches, lobs usually, and once B had been amused by them. But eventually I could see the corners of his lips tightening when I talked, and grew afraid to open mine except to say, "More salad, anyone?" and, "Oh, yes, I saw a good review of that in the _Times._"

Now, because I never gave and seldom went to dinner

parties (potential hosts, I figure, may have feared I might talk about "it"), I was usually alone, except for the children, with whoever was speaking to me. My daughters squeezed themselves between me and the guest. They lingered in doorways or, courting invisibility, secreted themselves on the stairs. They wanted to hear chatter, bathe in the sea of normality, and I was, in a sense, asleep. But my hearing was coming back, sharp enough for me to drown in dialogue, savor style. It was never sharper than on a June afternoon a few weeks after we had moved into our Anglo-Italianate stable.

I had been divorced (and B newly married) for four months, and was about to leave for Australia for the magazine. I was longing to go, longing to leave the Saturday night trio of Archie Bunker, Bob Newhart, and Mary Tyler Moore, and the hours behind my closed bedroom door reading and rereading Colette because I thought there were lessons to be learned there. I wanted to be someplace where there was no chance of meeting B and his new wife. Above all, I wanted to be someplace where nobody knew me and I could use my voice again.

But why were my ears so sharp on that particular June afternoon? Because I was listening to a woman named Lillian.

Two

The first time I met Lillian Roxon,
it was to hire her to write *Mademoiselle*'s (I was its managing editor) sex column. "Forgive the lounging pajamas," she said to me in her wild Australian nasal when we entered Cheval Blanc, a French restaurant not far from the Graybar Building and, at that time, one of countless just like it. They all served chilly pâtés, sole meunière, crème caramel, and featured mean-looking middle-aged women at the cash register. "The exterminator came this morning, and the bug bombs stank up everything else."

"Everything else" was a collection of strange floating robes home-dyed in colors like puce and mustard and fuchsia, and patched, wherever a seam had split, with Mickey Mouse fabric transfers. The cortisone Lillian took for asthma had made her buoyant as a waterbed, and, embarrassed by her fat, she had turned herself into a billboard that was fun to read and, since one was amused on seeing her, unpitiable. There was only one public place where she would bare her body, a rundown rooftop solarium at either Coney Island or Brighton Beach, where old Jewish women went to strip and sun. Here there was no reason for self-consciousness, no reason to hide what had happened to a body that had not yet touched forty.

Most of Lillian's friends, many of whom were rock stars and their groupies, were younger than she, and she was to them as she was to Snow White, a Rabelaisian sort of mother. Lillian sent my daughter funny notes in envelopes she'd watercolored and stuck with gilt stars. She gave her records — one of them of the singing squirrels and all of them "guaranteed to drive your mother up a wall" — and a lavender-painted strongbox because "every young girl should have one to lock up letters and diaries." When she came to call she always went to Snow White's room first, and I could hear them giggling behind the closed door. "I think I ought to tell you, Mary, just to set your mind at ease," she told me once. "If your daughter ever runs away from home — and don't tell her I told you this — don't worry. I made her promise to run away to me."

Mother to her friends, mother to my daughter, Lillian was, ironically, my child. She liked the order of my house — her apartment was as messy as a child's closet — and the way that meals appeared on time and rituals like Christmas and birthdays were faithfully observed. "You're so ladylike, so discreet, my dear," she teased. Sometimes she was too, or tried to be. She looked beautiful the night that, wearing pearls and a 1920s chiffon dress, she was hostess of an evening at the theater for an Australian playwright, and stood in the lobby greeting the guests and waving them in like a small and pretty Texas Guinan. Soon after I went into the auditorium, however, she slugged a woman who was crashing. After the play there was a party, and everyone congratulated Lillian on her right hook, but the evening had been ruined for her. She had dressed up, she had been a grand lady even, but a flick of her fist had turned her, in the eyes of the guests and of her disappointed self, into funny old Lillian again.

Some people leave their ghosts in rooms where they've been, so whenever my mind's eye sees Number 83, it also sees Lillian, sitting round as a Buddha on an angular twig chair or on the small rug next to the loveseat, gesturing with her glass of diet soda. She is talking about the woman she had slugged ("I had to, Mary. That little bitch had it in for me") and what she should wear to cover Tricia Nixon's wedding for the Australian news agency for which she worked ("I thought I'd go very Middle America, so I bought this kind of polyester shift at Lamston's and a white plastic purse that snaps shut. Do you think it'll do?") and why David Bowie's wife bit her ("I suppose she wanted attention") and another rocker's presumed genital measurements ("A lovely, lovely boy — bet you think that's naughty, Mary") and the day she'd get it together. "When I get it together, Mary, when I get it together, I'm going to Elizabeth Arden and I'm going to have a facial and a massage and a pedicure, the whole number." I loved her language and the way she spoke it, spun through the nose with a touch of Cockney. Mostly, though, I loved being able to have a friend who didn't have to pass B's taste test. Like most wives — most husbands too, I suppose — I had trotted out each new acquaintance as if it were a purchase sent on approval.

We were in the garden on this hot June afternoon because I had to go to Sydney. The magazine was involved in a promotion for Australian wool, and Lillian, who had lived there for most of her twenties, knew exactly whom I should see and whom I should avoid.

"If you're invited to meet ——, don't, I beg you, Mary, don't go. He'll come at you with those big teeth of his and he'll talk your ear off; and I know you, Mary. You'll be too polite to move away and you won't learn anything and you'll be covered with spit besides, because he sprays when he speaks.

"I'm only sorry you're going to miss G. Did I tell you her latest? She really wanted to fuck M" (Lillian named a famous American writer), "but he wasn't interested, so she picked up this cab driver. She had him around for about a week — he looked good you know; Italian — and she told everyone he was *muy macho*. But she told me he was a lousy lay. Then he split because he got bored, so she told everyone she'd had to dump him because he was so forceful she'd got vaginitis. My God, that woman's got a mouth. I felt like saying to her, 'But, G, how could he do that with a limp prick?'"

Lillian widened her eyes and covered her mouth when she saw I was blushing. "Oh, Mary, I keep forgetting I have to watch my language when I'm around you. Now to get to a cleaner subject, more your thing, Mary — there's a little antique shop, Kaleidoscope. And you must meet M.F. She's got a finger in every pie in Sydney. Not that Sydney's got that many pies, you understand."

I cannot remember saying goodbye any more than I can remember who took care of the children while I was gone. But I can picture the scene. My older daughter would have been stony-faced. The younger one would have been crying. I would have been poised at a midpoint between happiness and guilt, and promising to bring back souvenirs.

Sydney didn't provide much in the way of souvenirs, only kangaroo-fur change purses. Nor did it have many pies. Why else would I have been treated as the Messenger from the West, passed from hand to hand, usually by editors from Australian *Vogue*, as this week's novelty. "What's happening in New York?" I'd be asked. "What's happening in the theater?" "Have you ever been to Max's Kansas City?" On and on they went, endless questions from what seemed to me a coterie of displaced persons, uncertain of their place on this planet. When, desperate to maintain my unearned status as a cultural Colossus, I mentioned a Hopper show at the Museum of Modern Art that I hadn't even seen, a fellow guest said, "At last! A spontaneous mention of Edward Hopper in Australia!"

Lillian's friend M.F. gave a cocktail party for me, culling the guests from an address book as big as an accountant's ledger. "I think you should meet an anthropologist, don't you? And a politician, so I'll ask Gough Whitlam. I'll ask Barry Humphries, because he's got a big name here as a comic — does Edna Everage, you know. And, of course, you'll want an economist . . ." I was awed. Not even the mayor of New York could have summoned so fancy a group in so short a time, but, then, Australia was a very small pond, so small that its big frogs could be clustered on the pages of just one address book.

At the party, flashbulbs popped, the drinking and backbiting reminded me of Dublin, and one guest, flaunting what Australians called the cultural cringe, said grandly, "We're all copyists here." Soon everybody departed, my hostess included, and I was left in an empty house, looking for a phone to call a cab.

Out in the harbor the Opera House seemed to scud before the wind, like a schooner under full sail, but most of the buildings, my hotel included, and many of the shop signs evoked the England of Lilibet and Princess Margaret Rose. So did the women in their sensible shoes and practical coats and glazed gray hair, and the five-and-tens that at intervals announced a sale on counter six or counter eight and sent their customers scurrying through the aisles. I had always been infatuated with what I had read and seen of the 1930s — mostly in movies starring Fred Astaire and Ginger Rogers or James Cagney and Ruby Keeler — and now I was living in that decade, suddenly tranformed into my own mother.

The Rocks, where the first convict ships docked, hadn't yet become a cross between Williamsburg and Boston's Quincy Market, and the nearby streets through which I wandered, looking for antiques shops, seemed sinister and Dickensian. Kings Cross, Sydney's version of Times Square, was thronged with fresh-faced hookers just in from the country, and every inner suburb — sections, still, of Sydney but with names of their own — had a High Street, lined with greengrocers and butchers. All that was missing to remind me of London were red double-decker buses brandishing signs for Ty-Phoo tea. Then night came and, with it, stars that were in the wrong places and the realization that I had never been on soil so foreign. My ancestors' bones were scattered all over Great Britain and Europe, maybe even Asia and Africa and the Americas. But not here, not on this curious continent. Home seemed impossibly distant; the miles between this world and mine incalculable. Some people long for lovers; those people who are said to be the missing halves of their psyches. The missing half of my psyche was not a lover but two daughters, three cats, an obstreperous dog, and the six o'clock smell of lambchops broiling on a rack. In truth, it still is.

The promotion for Australian wool meant that, in the great fashion magazine tradition of rolling over and playing dead for potential advertisers, we were to devote several pages to a sheep ranch. So, with a photographer, a fashion editor, and a young New Zealander we saw in a park and who, with his fair hair and toothy grin, seemed to us as essential a photo-

graphic prop as an emu or a koala, I flew south to an aiport so
small that it was open only if you called ahead and asked
them to turn on the runway lights.

The ranch was miles from the airport, at the end of an
empty road that arrowed through rust-colored earth and
hard blue hills furred with dense green trees. It was like
driving through a void, but for the occasional interruption of
thick heavy birds that swooped, lumbered really, in front of
the car, stands of tall, thin ragged trees, and sudden clumps
of ugly, boxy buildings freighted with the elaborate ironwork
called Sydney lace. The light was unearthly, filtered through
pewter-colored clouds to sit on tiny towns that resembled sets
for a movie about the American frontier.

The ranch house was enormous, Victorian, a Nob Hill
monstrosity set in tangled grass and ringed with thousands
of sheep. Its owner and sole occupant was a young woman
who, when I asked if she was ever lonely, said, "Not when
I see this land, this space . . ." and flicked a hand toward
emptiness. My eyes followed her hand — she was pointing,
it seemed, at infinity — and at that moment I fell in love
with Australia. It was alien and yet it was not — when she
said, "We think nothing of driving one hundred miles to a
ball," I thought of Jane Austen — and, like the Wild West
of my Saturday afternoons at the movies, it promised the
impossible.

"You conquered your interior," a man at the cocktail
party had said, "but ours defeated us." "For God's sakes,"
another warned, "don't let yourself be talked into a flight
across the outback. The only diversion is spotting brush-
fires." But I had forgotten all that. I was besotted with the air
and the clarity and a silence that soothed like aloes.

The young woman and I talked all day, wrapped in the
peculiar intimacy of people who will never see each other

again, and walked among the small, silly sheep and the shearing sheds and men who looked like cigarette ads. At night we dined in a room as formal, as glossed with silver and slicked with china, as any Spreckels mansion, and the young New Zealander couldn't get over the pink linen napkins. "Pretty posh," he said, and watched to see how we settled ours on our laps.

The space. I had never been in such space. It should have made me feel small. It didn't. I felt magnified, and magnified even further by an image left me by a man whose letters I kept in the top drawer of my bureau. He had traveled through the outback, he said, and had met an aborigine carrying a didgeridoo, a wind instrument. He tuned his guitar to the didgeridoo, and they played together. It may have been a fiction — most of his stories were — but I didn't know that yet. Even so, I was suspicious. It was too good, too pat: civilized and primitive man meeting in a fugue. No matter. The image, combined with what I had seen myself, lifted me into the air, so high I was like the all-seeing eye on a dollar bill, scanning Australia, all Australia, all at once.

Then I came home and found Rose Red sad because I had missed her ninth birthday by one day. I doubt she has ever forgiven me, and I know I have never forgiven myself. There was nothing I could have done about it. The airline I was on, _had_ to be on, because again, in the great tradition of fashion magazines, the flight was a freebie — had only three or four flights a week to the United States. Still, I kept telling myself, I should have been there. I should have baked the cake. I should not have left her to be wet-eyed on the day she turned nine.

The letters in the top drawer of my bureau were from a writer whom I had asked to contribute a short piece to the magazine's book column. He did, and we embarked on a brief correspondence that grew, on his part, flirtatious. Maybe he liked the way I turned a phrase. More likely he thought that the former wife of a former acquaintance of his, a man who had punctured his ego by declining to work any longer with someone whose mendacity outweighed his considerable talents (B held no brief for the term "artistic license," no matter how craftily employed), might add a few imprecations to his own.

Eventually he wrote that he was going to be in New York for the weekend and could I have dinner. If I had heard unsavory things about him, and later I remembered I had, I disregarded them, so eager was I to talk about books and poetry. When I went to meet him one cold November night, an anthology of his work was hidden in my shoulder bag. If he was friendly, if he seemed nice, I was going to ask him to sign it for me.

There was a cab strike that week, and I'd had a long walk from the bus stop. The chilly air pinked my cheeks, made me prettier than usual, I suspect, because I saw his face light up when he saw me waiting by the house phones. My first sight of my husband — dark, wearing a raincoat, standing in the living room of my college dormitory — is etched on my mind. So is my first sight of this man, the famous writer: big, fair, balding (his back hair, which he'd let grow long, had been swept up on one side and brushed across his bare pate), in a bright blue suit whose paisley lining matched his tie.

I walked to meet him, extended my hand; he mumbled something and steered me to the dining room. Just as we were sliding into the banquette, he said, "Mary, you evah been screwed till ya screamed?"

Before I could reply (just as well, because I couldn't

have), he said, turning to face me, "Ah'm a womanizer. Ah just love them tight-assed little girls."

He described a few: assorted college sophomores ("They don't know nothin'"), a waitress in Lubbock, Texas ("Said ah was the finest man she evah knew"), a movie actress ("flat-chested but a good-time gal").

Perhaps I should have stopped my solitary (he was too busy talking to extend a helping hand) struggle with my coat. Perhaps I should have pulled it back onto my shoulders and flounced out the door. But I was titillated. Besides, I was carefully weaving a tale for the gang at the office. "Talk about feet of clay," I was going to tell them. "His clay feet went right up to his hips!" Too, as I had with the man who dared me to drink a full glass of Scotch, I wanted to prove to myself that I was tough, that I could take it, that nobody and nothing could faze me. So I chattered, I glissaded, skittish as a hog on ice.

"We don't need all this food," he said, pointing to my steak tartare. (In all the years we dined together I always ordered steak tartare because I was too nervous to chew.) "Come up to mah room. I've got a couple of six-packs on the windowsill." A loud laugh. "I call it the Pigeon Bar."

I dodged, and mentioned the magazine I worked for and how proud we were to have published him. "Ah love ladies' magazines," he said. "Mah wife's a fashion freak and she buys them all. And ah love them Zonite ads."

("Mary," a friend said the next day. "You didn't find him just a bit of an oaf?"

"No," I said defensively. "It's just that he says what everyone else is thinking.")

"You know what these are?" He reached into his pocket and dropped two pieces of metal on the table.

I picked them up. "Guitar picks?"

He was surprised. "You know anything about guitar?"

"A little," I said. "I have a lot of Doc Watson records and . . ." I dropped the small talk. "But what I really love is fado. Have you ever heard fado?"

I was off, forgetting to whom I was speaking, forgetting what he'd been suggesting, intent only on describing the music.

"Fado is a Portuguese word for, I guess, fate. And it describes a certain kind of song, a kind of wail. And the women who sing them are called *fadistas*. They sing about *saudade*, which is sorrow, but that's too narrow a definition. It means longing and loss and regret for what you haven't had and cannot even name, as well as for what you had that's gone.

"B and I used to hear fado in Lisbon. We went to Portugal twice and stayed in a little fishing village called Cascais — it's rather fancy now — and drove into the city almost every night to park our car near the Ritz Hotel. Then we'd take a cab downtown to the Alfama — that's a rabbit warren of narrow streets, the oldest part of Lisbon — for fado. We'd sit in a little room with benches and tables, and a man with a guitar would come out and perch on a stool. Then the *fadista* would appear and put a black shawl over her head and shoulders — they always put on a black shawl — and sing. It's like keening, Irish keening. You must get an Amalia Rodrigues record. She's the greatest *fadista* in Portugal."

On I went, my hands sketching the room and the night and the shawl dropping over the shoulders, out of New York and into Lisbon with my husband, excited and happy.

"Keep it up, mah Mary," he said. "You're lookin' good."

He quieted then. Maybe the bourbon he'd been drinking before he came down to the lobby — I didn't know he was a heavy drinker — had worn off. Maybe, though, what happened to him was what I saw happen many times later. He had run down. He was overexcited when he got to the city, overexcited when he saw a new face, overanxious to stamp himself on a person or a room so that she, even it, would know she had met someone.

He had performed so constantly, had so consciously constructed a public image, that he had erased his self. Maybe he had no self. Maybe to live he had to kill it. Maybe, too, his best work was behind him, so his next work, the one that would keep him busy for the rest of his life, was to create the legend he wanted to leave after himself.

For all his weight and height and boasts and booming voice, and the way he V'd his thin, pale eyebrows over his round blue eyes and drew back his lips over his tall, narrow teeth when he feigned anger, he was as insubstantial as the jack o'lantern he sometimes resembled. There was only one time when he was real, at least to me, and that time began when, after my description of the _fadistas_, we began capping one another's quotations. I was — we were? how can I speak for him? — as giddy as I had been on my first date with my first boyfriend when we discovered we both liked lemon Cokes.

"Dover Beach" turned out to be one of our favorite poems. We recited it, or tried to — neither of us had a good memory for verse — in alternating lines. We talked about Gerard Manley Hopkins, and I told him of how, when my younger daughter said she wanted to be "young in her youth," I thought of "Margaret, are you grieving / Over Goldengrove unleaving."

"There's a rather peculiar English woman I like, too," I said.

"I know. I know," he crowed. "'I was much too far out all my life . . .'"

"'And,'" I finished, "'Not waving, but drowning.'"

"Mah Mary," he said, putting his hand over mine, "I'll bet we're the only two people in New York who know that poem. You know what I like about you? You're mah equal. Mary Cantwell, we're gonna be one long thing."

It was late, and I had to walk to Ninth Avenue to find a bus, so I got up to leave. On our way through the lobby he said, "It's just as well you didn't come upstairs. I wouldn't have been much good to you."

"That wouldn't have mattered. I think I'd have been happy just to sleep beside you." Then, stunned by what I had said, I put my arms around his neck and kissed him.

The next day, when I told a friend about my dinner with this writer I had idolized, she laughed, as I hoped she would, especially when I aped the way our natural accents exaggerated themselves as we spoke to each other, his getting more Southern, mine more New England. Then — flushed, flustered, a little teary — I confessed how much his saying I was his equal meant to me.

In a month or so he called and said someday he'd take down my panty hose and give me a good spanking. My marriage had been to me analogous to entering a convent — I never strayed outside the grounds — so my response, silence, was as innocent as that of a child who, despite a thorough warning, was about to take candy from a stranger. Yet I was cautious enough not to use the ticket he sent me for a panel discussion he was chairing in New York. I wouldn't risk going alone. When I called him at his hotel and said I was sorry I couldn't be there and wished him luck, he said, "Mah Mary, you're always running away from what you really want." And when I told Dr. Franklin, the psychiatrist at whose office I had so often wept during the wake I was holding for B, about the writer's phone calls and the vulgarity that had me as mesmerized as a mongoose faced by a snake, he said, "Don't you go near that man."

But one day I did, because I thought he was life.

Three

During the long stretch between separation and divorce, I had read a lot. I had read about how much better it was for the children if an end was brought to an unhappy marriage. I had read that staying together for their sake was practically a crime against nature. I had made an appointment with B's psychiatrist, who seemed surprised when I said that two people who had brought children into the world had a responsibility toward them that surmounted their own petty concerns. "You're a real Christian!" he said, amazed. More likely, in the world in which B and I had lived for seventeen years, I was a real anomaly.

The house quiet but for the children's soft breathing and the occasional clunk from the radiator, I would steal from my bed and, sitting in the dark, humiliate myself with midnight phone calls. "Please," I would beg, "I can change. I can be anything you want me to be." Then, as usual, work saved me from being someone of whom my father would have been ashamed. (How he would feel about my self-abasement was ever on my mind and kept me poker-faced in public.)

Mademoiselle's guest editors, winners of a contest that would enable them to edit the August College Issue (most of which had been completed before they arrived), had as part of their prize a week in a foreign country. I had semi-chaperoned a previous group in Israel. I was escorting the new group to Ireland.

Most of my charges didn't like Ireland — the g.e.'s, as we called them, tended to judge countries by their shopping potential — and I was glad to be shot of them soon after we got to Dublin. The editor-in-chief called to say the magazine had got some unexpected advertising from Yugoslavia, and, lacking a quid pro quo, she wanted me to make a rush trip for a rush article. It was June, the children were out of school and in good hands, and I would have one more week away from a city in which I saw the ghosts of my husband and myself on every corner. I arrived in Yugoslavia armed with the entire *Forsyte Saga,* and soon found myself immersed in a London that seemed far more real than the cities and countryside about which I was assiduously making notes.

Still, I recall sitting on the ramparts that surround Dubrovnik and thinking that if I just leaned backward a bit, I would fall to a death that everyone would think accidental. At the same time I was uncomfortably aware of the small stones that were pocking my backside. "As long as your butt is counting pebbles, mah Mary," the balding man said when I told him of that momentary hover between feeling and oblivion, "I'm not gonna worry about you."

I recall, too, an old woman watching me from the window of a building bordering the restaurant terrace on which I was eating an early dinner, and that I raised my glass to her. And another woman, in white, with a pyramidal straw hat and the kind of honeyed skin and hair and slanty brown eyes I always associate with Hungarians, standing in a rose-choked fourteenth-century cloister. "Dubrovnik," she said. "There is nothing more beautiful, is there?" When I mentioned her charm to my guide, he shrugged. "I have seen her before," he told me. "She is mad."

I remember Belgrade, and how brown and sluggish the beautiful blue Danube was as it slouched past my hotel window, and an evening sitting with people from the tourist commission while all around us the other diners sang the Yugoslav equivalent of "You Are My Sunshine." I was wearing my wedding ring, still, as I saw it, under my husband's protection. I spoke of him, too, as if he were home waiting for me. Instead, he was to me as dead as Virginia Woolf's brother Thoby was truly dead all the time she was writing her friend Violet Dickinson about his temperature, his moods, his crossness with his nurses because they wouldn't give him mutton chops and beer. Even during the midnight phone calls that preceded my final letting go, I had recognized the man I was talking to as B's simulacrum. This man, who one night hissed "Cocksucker!" into my ear, could not be my husband.

I saw Germans, always recognizable because their shorts never quite covered their rumps, and coveys of Russians, the women all wearing the same kind of shoddy, low-heeled beige shoes, and elderly American women unconquered by their varicose veins and elastic bandages. I dined one afternoon on roast kid (I thought it was baby lamb), in what I was told was Tito's favorite restaurant, and one evening with a young man who idolized Albert Szent-Györgyi. When I spoke of Szent-Györgyi's having said that the world was a small cave we could not afford to litter, the boy looked at me with warm brown eyes and said, "You sound like a Yugoslav student."

Talking. I was talking all the time, because there was no Yugoslav who didn't want to practice his English and because I have the gift, if gift it is, of instant intimacy. Add up those moments when you and a stranger connect, I thought to myself, and you can turn them into a life for yourself.

The longest talk was with a middle-aged woman who was working for a new hotel on the Adriatic. The old town, settled by Bosnian Turks, was nearby, and we walked through threads of streets and the smell of sardines to a restaurant on the water, where she spoke of her two brothers and a sister-in-law who had been executed during World War II. She couldn't forget them, she said, but she had forgotten to hate. "We spend so much time looking inside ourselves that all we see is darkness. But if we look out — there is so much that is beautiful."

Ah, this is one of the good times, I said silently, this coming together with someone I would never see again, and both of us looked toward the sky, hunting the Big Bear and the Little Bear. But as we did I realized that my children, having grown up under a sky in which the only star one could rely upon was Venus, had never seen either, and I was sick with longing. No, this was not a life, this little accumulation of epiphanies, not a life for me.

Before I left Yugoslavia, however, there was another good time, in Split, which I liked because walking through it was like touring fifteen or so centuries at the same time. Bits and pieces of at least a thousand years of construction had been jumbled together into the architectural equivalent of a magpie's nest. Rome is also a magpie's nest, of course, but Rome is too big for me to swallow. Split was just my size.

I was wandering through a small church, mostly Byzantine, I think, and asking more questions than the guide, a girl no more than twenty, could answer. "Oh, this isn't fair to you," she said, and ran off to get the head guide, a tall thin man in his fifties, dressed all in white but for the black beret tilted over his thick gray hair. He was enormously well informed, and polished to a degree that Americans (sometimes I feel a part not only of a recently evolved country but of a recently evolved race) never attain, but I suspect he was also poor. Why else would a university professor, which he was, spend his summers trying to educate tourists like me into some quickly forgotten semblance of scholarship?

Was he married, I wondered, or a bachelor? Did he have a house, an apartment, or one small room? Did he find what he was doing demeaning? I wanted to burrow my way into his head, because I wanted to burrow my way into his life. I didn't know how to live mine; I didn't even know how to sit still. That was the real reason I traveled. It was a way to quiet the ants that were forever crawling under my skin. But I asked him nothing except the period of this fresco, the provenance of those curious columns, thanked him politely, tipped him nicely, and returned to Soames and Irene and London's damp chill.

It was the same when I got back to New York. I needed books so that I could live their characters' lives, not mine, and I needed rooms beyond the virginal white bedroom in which I sat, propped against pillows, a glass of slivovitz (my only souvenir of Yugoslavia) in my left hand and a book, any book, in my right. I was listening, to Virginia Woolf, to Jean Rhys, and, mostly, to Colette, whom I believed to be the font of all wisdom, not realizing that she, who wrote so movingly about solitude, scarcely had a solitary moment in her life.

Beyond my bedroom door was a windowless inner room good for nothing but a library, and here it was that I had imagined my children doing their homework when they were old enough for it, at the big center table under the green-shaded hanging lamp. But when the time came, Rose Red did her homework wherever I was, and Snow White did no homework at all.

Their rooms were on the other side of the library, Snow White's strewn with strange caches of dirty glasses and gum wrappers and notes passed at school, letters from people barely met, and Janis Joplin records. Already, she had a passion for the doomed and the dramatic and would put on a long pink dress and tie a homemade black velvet choker around her neck on Sunday nights to watch the _Masterpiece Theatre_ shows about Henry VIII, Elizabeth I, and their courts. Above all, she was obsessed with Anne Frank, whose diary she read over and over again. She identified with Anne Frank, she said. Anne Frank was her best friend.

Rose Red's room was neat, with a dollhouse, stuffed animals on the bed, birthday cards taped to the wall, and a small electric organ and miniature bottles and a soap collection and a candle collection and stacks of Archie comics. When the girls were small, I had sat in the room with bunny wallpaper and told them stories and sung "Rock-a-Bye, Baby." Now, with the streetlight shining in my window and the garden dark beneath theirs, we stayed apart too many nights, Snow White with Anne Frank and Rose Red with her Archies and I with my books, my wonderful books, which all my life had arisen and engulfed me in a reality more powerful than my own. When I was a child, immersion in a book deafened me to calls to come to the dinner table, help dry the dishes, get ready for bed. Now, at night, books deafened me to soundlessness — a phone that didn't ring, a door that would never open again to bring my husband home. But I _could_ hear Daisy Buchanan weeping over Jay Gatsby's shirts, and Lord Peter Wimsey wooing Harriet Vane with John Donne.

Rose Red, determined to be "young in her youth," was also determined that I provide her with a childhood. If I came home from work tired and thinking about sandwiches, she would say, "It's a mother's responsibility to give her child hot meals," and send me, my exhaustion suddenly erased by her demands for order, to the kitchen. Out they would come, the linguine with clam sauce and the salad, and there my daughters would sit, the one lazily forking her pasta and the other grinning triumphantly.

We worked on her dollhouse together — one summer weekend when my mother was visiting, she and I had wallpapered all its rooms — and sometimes Rose Red and I spent long hours after supper with intricately detailed coloring books and colored pencils, each of us busily and quietly turning out fantastically ornate Elizabethan court dresses. The day she talked me into washing the clothes of her Meg, Jo, Beth, and Amy dolls and painstakingly ironing them, she watched from my bed, blissful because her mother was doing what a mother was supposed to do. As a baby she never tried to climb out of her playpen the way Snow White did, and, later, she never sat on a chair without first testing its strength with a timorous hand. Her ear was finely tuned to the moment of ripeness, and not until she heard it would she move on.

I was, and remain, grateful for her bossiness. In guarding her childhood, she was also guarding my motherhood. Too, she had my grandmother's earthiness — my grandmother, whom I once saw carry a live water rat by its tail to the backyard incinerator, and who inevitably uttered, "The old goat!" when a widower went courting. One evening Rose Red and I were cooling ourselves at my bedroom window when a car stopped directly under the streetlight. The passenger — male or female I do not know, because the nearby meat market was thick with transvestite prostitutes — promptly unzipped the driver's fly, then buried her head in his lap. Rose Red ran from the room, in shock I assumed, to come back a minute or so later with her bird-watching binoculars. After carefully adjusting the sights, she trained them on the couple and howled, "Mom, they're corrupting me!"

Snow White, though, didn't want to be young. Snow White wanted to grow up very fast, because adulthood — sixteen years old, anyway — meant emancipation. I had cried over B and now I cried over her, wondering what made my husband and now my daughter want to run away from me. That it may have been something in them and not something in me never entered my mind, so convinced was I of my power to destroy.

Even so, there were moments, like the evening the two of us went to the theater and Snow White, wearing her best gingham dress, asked why people didn't dress up for great occasions like this one. I commiserated; I agreed; we were partners in condescension. There was another evening when someone had given me house seats for the Royal Ballet and we sat next to an old woman draped in diamonds, whom I recognized as the mother of a famous murderee, and her escort, the usual young man in the usual tasseled Gucci loafers. Snow White couldn't see the stage for the diamonds, and finally asked the old woman if they were real. "Oh, yes," the woman said, and held out her braceleted arm for inspection. We were happy that night, she a child again and I a mother with a foolish, apologetic grin. She let me tuck her in for the first time in months when we got home — Rose Red was already asleep — and I thought of Sylvia Plath's poem about the dead woman who has folded her dead children "back into her body as petals / Of a rose close when the garden / Stiffens . . ." I would never wish my children dead, as I often did myself, but I knew all about wanting to fold them back into my body, where I could keep them safe and warm forever.

"Mah Mary," the balding man said, angry because his rare evening in New York was being ruined by the pain in my head, "you'd better do something about those headaches."

But I had. After their onset, when I was twenty-three, I had sat for years in a psychiatrist's office, because a doctor had told me therapy would cure migraine. It didn't. It doesn't.

The headaches came without warning; they were unavoidable, because I couldn't analyze their cause, and they usually left me crying and helpless for three days. More destructive than the pain, however, was the contempt I — and B, too — felt for me. I had read that personality was responsible for migraine, that it was the punishment accorded perfectionists and the high-strung, people who could not take criticism or confrontation. Once again I was proving myself impossible, and I could hear B's impatience in the balding man's voice. Perhaps a Bronx hospital's headache unit that I had just heard of might be helpful. Perhaps the doctor who had said I had migraine and sent me to a psychiatrist had made a misdiagnosis. Perhaps, I thought, hopeful because I didn't realize the seriousness of the alternative with which I was presenting myself, I had a brain lesion.

Week after week I took a long subway trip and a long walk to the hospital, to sit in a waiting room crammed with people who had whatever it was I had. There were small children there, and middle-aged men, and people who were dressed nicely, and people who were dressed poorly. Rather than the isolated neurotic I'd believed myself to be, it appeared I was part of a community of sufferers, and that knowledge was more useful than any of the countless ergo-tamine tablets I had swallowed over the years.

The tests, none of which I had had before, seemed end-less. At the end of them the doctor, a young Filipino whose hair was as black and as stiff as the bristles on a clothes brush, said, "You have common migraine."

"Oh, God," I said to myself, "he's going to send me to another psychiatrist." I could see them all beginning again: the tears when I spoke of my father, who had betrayed me by dying, the tears when I spoke of B, who had betrayed me by loving someone else, the endless circling between my child-hood and the present, and no exit from the pain in my head.

"You probably inherited it," he added.

A set of swollen arteries, as inevitable to a Cantwell as a prognathous jaw to a Hapsburg, had been handed down from generation to generation. For the pain in my head I'd been declared "not guilty."

"Your personality didn't create the pain. The pain cre-ated your personality," the doctor said. I should have been joyous. Instead, I was enraged. But for that cluster of aber-rant arteries (not my fault, not my fault), I was normal. Yet for years, several doctors, countless magazine articles, my husband, and myself had told me that, in one respect at least, I was not.

To be normal. I became infatuated with normality, asked doggedly that it be defined, and measured myself against the definition. When a doctor told me that my blood chemistry fit "the textbook definition of normal," I bragged. My blood pressure, a steady 120 over 80, enchanted me. If I could have, I would have papered a room with the results of my Pap smears. All said, "No abnormal cells." It was not so much that I feared cancer as that I loved having a cervix that was lined with innocence. Others were enthusiastic about their abnormalities; I, about my normalities. I was crazy about my cholesterol count.

Heterosexuality, however, defeated me. I could not construct a norm. B was the first naked man I had ever seen, and when I did, I thought of Jesus in His drooping loincloth. Surrounded by an iconography that showed God as a man, my sexual associations were religious, and what I wanted from sex, when finally I did want something from it besides babies, was Communion. Is that normal? History, pyschology, and a millennium or two of literature say no.

It is October. I love October. It makes me think I am in school and that I have homework and that my father and I are going to tune in *Inner Sanctum* and turn out the lights so that he can scare my sister and me with odd whistles and tappings. We still exchange memories of him, very different memories, because I knew one man and she knew another. The father I knew was pleased that I shared his bookishness and the joy he took in language, and he smiled whenever he heard me intoning, as he so often did, "Had I the heaven's embroider'd cloths . . ." Diana's father was enchanted by the eagerness with which she embraced swimming and softball and basketball, and he once had high-topped sneakers — she had weak ankles — made just for her. But whenever we speak of Papa, the identical smile lights our faces.

It is October, and I am on my way to a cocktail party with the balding man. He doesn't want to go, but I have promised — it is the first time the hostess has entertained since her husband died — so he is sitting half-drunk in a corner of the cab and he is sniping at me.

"You've got a mean, intelligent face."

I am silent.

"Mary Cantwell, the clock is running out on you."

"That depends on what clock you're watching," I say calmly. I have the resilience of a roach.

We get to the party and he stalks through it like an angry bear. He isn't rude, but he's showing off, and he's feeding so visibly on the adulation of his fans that he's swelling like the corpse in the Ionesco story who gradually swallowed up the room.

The hostess and a friend from the office take me aside. "Mary, stay here with us," she says. "You can't leave with that man," he says. "They'll be picking you up in bits and pieces all over Riverside Drive tomorrow."

"I have to go," I say, because I have made up my mind. I cannot bear any more dreams about B, and half-waking with my arms half-open. If this man is the sexual giant he has claimed to be during the year since we met, he is going to blast me right out of those nightmares. The children are away for the weekend, and I have put my best sheets on the bed.

I take his arm and we go to a dinner party, where none of the guests speak to him because he is drunk and because they dislike him.

"Mah Mary," he says, "please don't let me drink. I don't want to make a fool of myself."

So I don't, happy to be needed, happy to mother, and he goes off, to sit in a corner like a schoolboy with a dunce cap and sober up. The moderator of the panel on which the males of this distinguished group, all of whom have written for the screen, are to speak later, leans over and says, "Don't you go in for the Madonna Dolorosa. You've got the face for it."

I laugh. This is the light, skinny chatter I enjoy at dinner parties, and he and I sparkle right through dessert.

While the other panelists are drinking coffee, the balding man and I walk around the block. He is sober now, and he is unhappy.

"Mah Mary," he says, "last night I was in Chicago, at a forum, and they offered me a woman. And I didn't want her, I didn't want her, but I took her because she was _offered_ me. I feel dirty."

If he had been B, the confession would have made me heartsick. But B was real, whereas the balding man is an actor. An autumn night in New York, an empty street, a pretty, rather innocent listener, and, in a few minutes, an audience of at least a thousand: how resist the chance to speak such compelling lines? But if he is an actor, so too am I. Playing the Madonna Dolorosa suits me very well.

At the theater, where the panelists are to speak after a movie screening, I sit in what I immediately christen Mistresses' Row. Each and every one of these pretty women who had been guests at the dinner, each of whom clearly has a camel's hair coat and the Yale Bowl in her past, is sleeping with one of these men, some of whom are married, up there on stage. I do not like this. I have been a wife too long to like being lumped with girlfriends.

Actually, I don't like anything about the evening, because the panelists, eager to prove why they had earned a place on a stage, are speaking mostly to their peers and hardly ever to the audience. True, one of them announces he has a good Sam Peckinpah story. But he forgets to tell it.

An hour or so later, after the panel breaks up, the balding man and I are leaving the theater when a young man steps out of a shadowed doorway and says, "I've been waiting here, sir, to tell you how much I admire your work."

I look across Lincoln Center, which by this hour is empty, at the fountain, still sending sprays of water into the midnight air, and at the young man hurrying off into the darkness. Awed by fame and, in this great plaza, its perfect setting, I ask, "Doesn't that make up for everything?"

"No," he says, and I marvel at the despair that too many years of reading biographies of Hemingway and Fitzgerald have convinced me attends genius. Anyone emerging from a shadowed doorway to say he had admired, say, my piece on Yugoslavia would have had me soaring.

We are in my living room now, and he, used to hotel rooms and probably afraid his wife will call and catch him out, says, "This isn't right, my bein' in your house."

"If it isn't right in my house, it isn't right anywhere," I say, and lead him upstairs. Propped on pillows, wearing my best nightgown, quiet, self-possessed, watching him fold his clothes on an old rocker, extending my arms when he turns and says, "Well, this is me," no one would ever guess that he is only the second man I have ever slept with.

"You don't feel any shame at all, do you?" he asks the next morning.

"No," I answer, "only joy," and I think he is disappointed. He has written about the magic of guilt, but guilt is magic only to the amateur. I think myself my husband's killer, and in indulging the balding man and his sad semblance of lust, I am not committing another crime but doing penance for the first.

When we part in front of his hotel and, restless, I walk through Bloomingdale's, I am too dazed to shop, and go home to slide between the sheets he's just vacated. I feel as though I've given birth to him, and that the umbilical cord still connects us. Dr. Franklin says, reluctantly, "I guess you won't feel so alone anymore." And I don't, not for years.

Four

The last time I saw the Snow White
I had known from the day she was born was on a Christmas
morning. We had opened the presents, and in a few minutes
her father was to ring the bell — he never entered the house
and I never entered the hallway to greet him — and take the
children to the country for the holidays.

Actually, it is not the sight of her that I remember as
well as I do the sharpness of her thin thighs. She was sitting
on my lap, crying, because going away meant Christmas
afternoon would be no turkey stuffed with chestnuts, no
guests applauding when I came out with the plum pudding,
no sitting past bedtime under the tree while I marveled at
the stool she had made for me in shop and the handkerchief
on which Rose Red had, in running stitch, embroidered my
name. Perhaps what she was going to would be more fun,
more filled with family, because her stepmother had many
relatives, and we were only three. But one thing, perhaps the
only thing, I know about children is that they are as wedded
to ritual as old priests are to the Latin Mass.

The doorbell rang. Rose Red, dry-eyed, lips set, already
the mother I was not sure how to be, took Snow White's
hand and walked her to the door. I never saw my elder child

again. Her semblance, yes, but never that same little girl. People are fond of saying that babies change from week to week. Go away for a few days and you come back to a whole other person. But it is not only infants that mutate. So do children, and while I was not watching, Snow White turned into someone I had not met before. Her younger self is present now only in old albums, in photographs where she stares at the world with wide wondering eyes, often with a flower — she loved to smell flowers — clutched in her small, short-fingered hand.

After the car drove off, I moved away from the curtains, around which I'd been peering, and allowed myself to cry. But not for long. I had to take down the tree, lug it to the gutter, and put away the ornaments for another, better year. Then I had to pack.

A few weeks earlier I had been in my office, working late. In truth, I didn't really need to work late. But I knew the nice young woman from Dominica who came in every afternoon so as to be there when the children came home from school — I could no longer afford a housekeeper — would stay until I got home, and here, in this office, was peace and order. Here I knew what to do, to move papers from In boxes to Out boxes, to sign my name to requisitions, to scribble in the margins of manuscripts that this paragraph here, that sentence there, needed more work. At Number 83, I did not. Perhaps I might say something to offend my daughters. Even worse, during our rare phone conversations, I might say something to offend B, whose contempt had a razor's edge.

I thought I was alone, so was surprised when the travel editor poked her head in my door. She had just got a promise of advertising from three different countries, but here it was, the Christmas season, and who on earth could she find to write the articles that would be the quid pro quo? I asked which countries, and when she mentioned Turkey, I said, "I'll go."

I would have gone anywhere, really, to escape a house that would be empty by Christmas afternoon and a Christmas tree that by the evening would be lying naked in a gutter. Going to Turkey meant fleeing absences — the smell of a roasting bird, the rustle of tissue paper — to embrace new presences. When I left, in the early evening, to deposit Fred at a friend's apartment until she could take him to a kennel the next morning, I felt as if I were closing the door on a tomb.

To enter my friend's apartment was to be surrounded by safety, because she was a woman who never took a risk. She hadn't risked marriage; she hadn't risked job-hopping; she hadn't even risked falling in love unless the man was a homosexual — closeted, of course. It was the era of the bachelor, the man-about-town, the always reliable escort to the Junior League Ball, and never did I, nor she, associate such a cadre with what we knew, for sure, were "fairies" or "the boys." We thought they were simply bachelors, in the sense that my grandfather's somewhat eccentric brothers had been bachelors, and assumed that somewhere out there were the someones who could catch them someday.

Oh, but it was so cozy in her apartment, she with her afterdinner framboise and her escort of the moment with his. The living room was strewn, but artfully, with discarded wrap and ribbons; a fire burned in the fireplace; Christmas ornaments — little birds, all of them — glinted on the mantelpiece. I didn't want to leave this pleasant room, these pleasant people, and Fred, who, scenting departure, tried to get in my lap and who, when at last I walked toward the door, hurled himself against my legs. But once in a cab, free of his howls and slicing through Queens, my calves were as tensed as a sprinter's before the pistol shot. Takeoff, and I wished I were lashed to the plane's nose like the figurehead on a ship, and soaring.

The smell of coal smoke: that's what woke me every morning in Istanbul, that and the sound of boats hooting on the Bosporus. The hotel was old fashioned, an Edwardian relic, and my room so dimly lit that the only place I could read was the bathroom. At night I lined the tub with a blanket, put some pillows at one end, and climbed in quite happily, surrounded by a space as bright and white as an operating theater. This time I wasn't traveling with Galsworthy. This time it was Edmund Wilson.

Because the hotel was well off the American tourist route, its guests were the few Turks who traveled, families mostly, European businessmen whose expense accounts did not permit first-class accommodations, and a lone middle-aged woman who, one night in the dining room, started talking in I do not know what language and left the table in tears.

It was the kind of dining room that encouraged tears, because its good days, had there ever been any, were long ago and its revelers were long since dead. The room was cavernous, as big as the dining salon of an ocean liner, and a pianist played old show tunes — "I'm Gonna Wash That Man Right out of My Hair," "People Will Say We're in Love" — in a skinny forest of potted palms down by the kitchen door. Unless some member of the Tourist Board had been appointed to show me Istanbul by night, I dined there every evening, drinking my white wine and eating my lemon sole and thinking myself a woman of the world, no longer myself but a character out of Graham Greene. When I slept, there were no more nightmares. The silence was like a sable brush that someone had stroked me with from head to foot, and in the morning, when I left my bed, I was as sealed as an egg.

Most of the hotels were in the new city, but most of what I wanted to see was in the old city, so every morning, through the fog, I would cross the Galata Bridge, through a clutter of cars and buses and horse-drawn carts, to a spider's web of streets. In retrospect, I don't know how I got there, because I was too shy to hail a *dolmus*, a kind of cab with assigned stops, and certainly I didn't dare the city buses, so I suppose I walked. In strange cities I have always walked, everywhere, with more trust in my feet and a map than in any car or driver. Too, my lack of languages (French, my only other, I mispronounce and misuse) makes me feel as if I have a rubber plug in my mouth, the kind that stops up sinks. So, lost more often than not, I have walked and walked, my mouth closed over my useless tongue, and never have I failed to get where I was going.

I walked to Sancta Sophia, where a fragment — only the heads are whole — of a mosaic of Saint John and Mary pleading with Jesus for the world's sinners induced a kind of melting, like a wound draining. I walked to the Blue Mosque, paved with a faience so blue, it stabbed the eye, and, shoeless on demand, I wondered at the equality that prevails when you and everyone around you are padding around in stocking feet. There was another mosque, the Quarye, whose mosaics evoked Yeats's "Sailing to Byzantium" as surely as if he were whispering it in my ear. I had loved Yeats in college, even used him as a kind of sex manual. "For love has pitched its mansion in the place of excrement," I would murmur over and over, trying to turn the awkward college couplings in B's car — my back pinioned by the steering wheel and my

53

legs splayed — into something resembling passion, ardor, romance.

"My God, we've sent a claustrophobe to the Grand Bazaar," the executive editor called out to _Mademoiselle_'s editor-in-chief when I phoned to report on the horror of walking through acres of embroidered robes and rugs, stacks of brass trays, and thousands of gold bangles, all of them illumined by fluorescent lights so bright they hurt my eyes. It was good to be able to speak English, even better to think of the gang back at the office fielding hyperboles and getting breathless over Anne Klein. If I was serious about doing my work well, I was wholly unserious about the work itself. It made me laugh too hard.

"Buona sera" and _"Quelle belle femme,"_ the dusty-looking young men would mutter as I walked by. (I suppose they would have muttered something in German had I been fair.) The American young men — one could tell them by their jeans and their godawful sandals — never said anything. They were too busy looking for hashish. "They seem to have an idea about the city," said a young girl the Tourist Board had made my luncheon companion as we were dining in a restaurant on top of the Galata Tower. It was wonderful talking again — about her university, her rent, and the one thing about the United States she really wanted to know. "What do you think of Jackie Kennedy now that she's married that Greek?"

Mostly, though, I was alone. I was alone the morning I took a crowded ferry across the Bosporus to Uskudar to see nineteenth-century houses that looked like weathered matchsticks, and an old Moslem cemetery pinned with cypresses and thick with tall tombstones that tottered drunkenly and seemed to leer at passersby. They seemed human, those tombstones, because their finials told me whether those beneath them had been men or women. "I am in Asia," I said to myself, awed that my own two feet had taken me so far. Perhaps I too could be a Freya Stark, wandering the Middle East, spying the past beneath the present.

But of course I could not be a Freya Stark, and not because I had two children and a tongue that could not twist itself around the unfamiliar. I could not be a Freya Stark because that night, dining at the best restaurant in Istanbul with people from the Tourist Board, I realized that this world, where tablecloths were spanking white and waiters dipped their trays to one's left, was truly my world. When we stopped on the long drive back to my hotel to buy huge circles of flat, crackly pastry from an old woman in a little lighted stand, alone in miles of dark, I shuddered at her isolation, imagining myself into her role as easily as I had imagined myself into that of a divorced housewife looking for lust at that roadhouse near the Long Island Expressway. At the same time, though, I reveled in my own solitude, because for once I was free of the baggage I'd been toting since, fresh out of school, I married a young man who once kept a copy of _Orlando_ in his trenchcoat pocket. A stranger to the country, a stranger to the people who carted me about, I was to the Turks only a woman with brown eyes, a big shoulder bag, and an almost unimaginable life thousands of miles away. To me, I was only myself, an integer again.

"No, no," the Turkish tourist office in New York had said when I offered a rough idea of my itinerary after Istanbul. "You musn't be in Ankara on New Year's Eve. Ankara is a city of civil servants. It will be deserted, and you will be lonely."

B and I had celebrated New Year's Eve only twice that I can remember, and I'd never done so in childhood. At home, my parents out for the evening, I would think deep thoughts and inscribe them in my diary, one of the several little spiral-bound notebooks I would buy during the year, write in for a month or two, then forget about. So New Year's Eve in an empty Ankara, me reading in bed and turning out the light before midnight, would be no different from all my New Year's Eves. But no, the nice tourist people said. "You must go to Izmir for the celebration. You will be happy there."

My escort, from the Tourist Board, was a plump, curly-haired man in his thirties who called me "Mees Mary" and ended his sentences with "et cetera, et cetera, et cetera," like the king in *The King and I.* As oily and ingratiating as a seal, he was also anti-Semitic. "What can you expect? They're Jews," he said when the noise from an adjoining table drowned our conversation. I bit my tongue, knowing that I of all people — the ex-wife of a Jew, the mother of two half-Jewish children — should snap back at him. But courtesy, as always, made a coward of me, courtesy and the one habit, apart from liking to polish silver, that I had inherited from my mother. We were too much given to making excuses for others, too willing to overlook the unspeakable. I outgrew the habit. She, however, has been a "lady" all her long life.

We ate fresh sturgeon on skewers, snatched, he said, "from under the noses of the Greeks," then went to the "number one deluxe nightclub," which was on top of the hotel. I doubt he could have afforded such a place if he hadn't had to take me about, so I imagine he may have thrilled to the belly dancer, the four female violinists sizzling through "Play, Gypsy, Dance, Gypsy," the four male Paraguayans singing Italian standards, and the black-satined blonde breathing "Mammy Blue." But maybe not. Maybe he would have liked to be at home with his wife and children, assuming he had any, drinking _raki_ and munching on pistachios. Or maybe he would have liked to be one of those men out on the dance floor, lean men with faces like hawks, dancing with women as plump and lush as overblown peonies. When the women, presumably their wives, returned to their tables, the men danced together, as I had seen Jewish men dance the hora, and it was then that I saw joy, only then that I saw love.

From Izmir on I traveled with a young Turkish woman just out of university and reluctant to marry, because she worried about her freedom. As we drove toward a coastal resort named Marmaris, I would look from her, dressed in imitation Pucci and teetering in high-heeled pumps, to the women I saw in yashmaks, layers of sweaters, and billowy pantaloons, bent double under bundles of branches or the fat, shawled children they were piggybacking (the men meanwhile were sitting in tilted-back chairs in every café doorway, under every tree), and wonder which of us she was more like.

I found out the afternoon we stopped at a camel fight we'd seen from the road. Past the veiled women standing on the walls surrounding the field we marched — she a monument to emancipation — straight to a pair of folding chairs some grinning men had set up for us in the front row. The camels were dressed to their long teeth in trappings shining with sequins, pearls, and gold embroidery, and blew bubbles through their fat pink lips. Their rear legs splayed, their stubby tails swinging, they seemed a peaceful lot until their keepers goaded them into halfhearted combat. Suddenly, one broke loose from its leading strings and chased me, the guide, and fifteen or twenty small boys from the field. Once, when I had longed for the Europe that Hemingway had known in the 1920s and whose footsteps B, like every junior-

year-abroad student of the 1950s, had retraced, I thought
that running the bulls at Pamplona would be _it._ I never had,
and now I would never have to. Running a camel was terrifying, and, better yet, I didn't know anyone else who had
done it.

We were terrified that night, too, in a hotel where we
were the only guests. A man had knocked at the guide's door,
saying he was the bellboy, and asked whether she had received her luggage. Since the hotel was empty, there was no
possibility of confusion about the luggage, so she, unnerved,
called the desk, only to get the same voice on the phone. This
time, however, he said he was the night clerk.

We were two miles from town, the man was prowling
about outside her room, and she, crying, wanted to sleep in
mine. I pushed a big chair against the door, got out my Swiss
Army knife, decided I could, if necessary, shinny down the
balcony — we were on the second floor — and go for help.

For weeks, I, who had been a Cerberus to my children,
had been responsible for no one but myself, for whom I was
never brave (except at work) about mounting a defense. But
now, with someone to protect, I was ready, even eager to test
my guts. I sat up all night, my hands poised for violence,
courageous because I was needed. Then morning came, and
with it a covey of cleaning women, and we moved on.

There was more horror to come, in a toilet in the town of
Mugla, from which we both emerged pale and gasping. It
was on the second floor of a restaurant — a man was posted
at the foot of the stairs to hand out paper napkins — and
served both men and women, though not, I prefer to think,
together. The toilet was a big room with a slanted floor that
had been segmented into narrow alleys down which water
flowed. One squatted at the head of an alley to evacuate,
then watched while whatever emerged floated to the foot,

where presumably it dropped into some kind of sewer. Several turds in the adjoining alleys had been becalmed along the way, however, and the smell and sight were well beyond what I recalled from Girl Scout latrines. "How are we to have tourism if nothing is done about the toilets?" the guide moaned once we were outside, dousing ourselves from the bottle of lavender water she kept in the glove compartment of her car. We laughed, then, friends who had been in peril of prowlers, runaway camels, and marooned turds, and today I cannot remember her name or her face.

Sometimes, however, I must have traveled alone, though never without a driver. With him, most of the time, I sat in silence, because I cannot remember anyone being with me in a small hotel in Bodrum except the five shawled women I used to sit with every night in the tiny lobby. It had a coal stove, on which a pot of marmalade was forever simmering, and we crowded around it — me reading, they knitting and chatting. We could not speak, but we smiled at one another often, free to do so because we were all female. I would never have smiled at a strange man in Turkey, and any upward curve of a Turkish woman's lips was hidden outdoors by her yashmak. But in this tiny lobby, with its smell of coal and oranges, we shared a shelter that was less a matter of bricks and mortar or wood and nails than of mutual femininity. But no. Femininity is not the right word. Femaleness. We were creatures of our bodies in a way that men can never be, equally fearful of infertility, equally fearful of childbirth, equally fearful of the lump in the breast or the bloody flux. We knew one another without ever having to open our mouths.

I was also alone when I went to Priene, a Greek ruin not far from Ephesus, set on a plateau above the Menderes River.

59

The climb to the ruin, along a steep path, was lung-cracking, but not as difficult as Freya Stark's route. In her time — I think it was the 1920s — there was no path to Priene, and one had to cross the Menderes and climb that side of the hill which faced it. Heavy rains had swelled the river, so she spent several days on the low-roofed second floor of a fisherman's cottage before she could cross, speaking to no one, eating whatever the fisherman's wife set before her. Purgatory and silence before Priene: I was envious.

It was very quiet on the plateau, and, but for the quick green of licorice plants, the only color — of the sky, the grasses, the ruins — was a pale cool gray. I hopped from toppled stone to toppled stone, watching for the snakes I had been told lived among them, and listening to the dull thunk of a sheep's bell in the distance. The stillness was crystalline, and I fantasized coming here again someday and sharing it with the balding man. So I picked up a small marble shard, assured myself that it was of no archaeological value whatever, and decided to bring it home to him. Now I should love to be able to run my fingers over that worn vestige of egg-and-dart molding, but at the time I could think only of how much more complete I would feel if I could once more give a present — apart from the necktie I chose every Christmas for my brother-in-law — to a man. For years I had pondered over what to give B for his birthday and Christmas, Valentine's Day even, and his shirt size — 16½–34 — was written on my heart. But divorce meant an end to Brooks Brothers, an end to secondhand bookstores for old Joseph Mitchells and Berton Rouechés, an end to leaning toward a salesman as I would toward a priest in a confessional and saying, "My husband wears pajamas, but I was thinking a nightshirt might be fun."

Ephesus was near Priene, acres of white marble splintered by the light and, unlike most archaeological digs, accessible to the amateur's eye. One could walk past the library, the temples, the priest's house, the sailor's brothel, the theater, with its two thousand-year-old seats, and actually _see_ them. Paul, upon whom I was prone to pile half my problems with Catholicism and with sex, preached here; Saint John is buried here, under a sixth-century basilica; and not far away, it is claimed, is Mary.

Mary's house, or at least the foundations of somebody's first-century shelter, was a little Lourdes, full of discarded crutches and framed prayers of thanks. Desperate as always to sniff the odor of sanctity, I breathed deeply of the room, waiting — as I had ever since the days when I knelt in the attic in Bristol praying to my Aunt Margaret, who, since she had died at eleven, I believed must be a saint — to sense a presence. None came, any more than an answer came after I had scribbled a plea that my husband not go away and stuck the paper in Jerusalem's Wailing Wall. So once more I lost my faith in prayer at the same time as, remembering a phallus-shaped stone in Bodrum and a nearby tree from which fluttered rags symbolizing cries to Allah from barren women, I retained my belief in magic.

It was that faith in magic which had me photographing Mary's house with my Brownie Starmite and eventually giving the pictures to the deeply religious Polish woman who often babysat for the children. She was very old, and tears came easily to her, so she cried when I gave them to her. "You make me so happy," she said, her tongue thickened by her accent and her sobs. "Now I know I work in a good Catholic home."

I am, as I have said, proud of my memory, which lays tenacious monkey fingers on much I would rather forget. Still, it has the occasional hole out of which I can pull nothing, not even the slightest wisp of a meeting or a journey. So all I know of Ankara is waiting, with a mustachioed Kurdish driver, outside an apartment house that looked like mud huts set upon mud huts. From it emerged my interpreter, a young man immaculately suited and tied and faintly ashamed of my having seen where he lived.

We drove east, toward the Valley of the Göreme, skirting a big salt lake to enter a landscape that was all beige and gray, occasionally spiked with black. A few more hours through naked, wrinkled hills, and we were in Nevşehir, a town of a desolation so complete, I was forever finding a reason to wander its scabbed streets. Dust flew up in our faces and hung in the air. The girls in the town brothel, the young man told me, made seventy cents a customer.

We were in Nevşehir because it had the only hotel near the valley that was open in winter, and we were the only guests, apart from some prospective guides who were there for training.

At sunset the air chilled, my radiator, a cheap English plug-in, didn't work, and the manager, realizing that I was freezing in my room and longing for the moment when I could sit in the dining room beside the flaming spits, set in the wall, for _doner kebab_, would invite me to his stuffy, overheated office for a drink. We had pistachios and a bottle of Johnny Walker and listened to Turkish 45s played on a small portable, and, although I couldn't speak to him, his wife, his three harum-scarum children, and the covey of guides, each of us falling over one another's feet, it didn't matter, because when you're eating and drinking and listening to music, talk becomes redundant. Later, after dinner, I would crawl into one of my room's twin beds, heap it with the blankets from the other, position the lamp with its forty-watt bulb on a pile of books, and open Edmund Wilson's *Classics and Commercials.* Outside, dogs racketed in the desert. Inside, my toes wriggled ever deeper into the blankets and I thought of how seldom I was lonely in the country. There was nothing here but me and the dogs and the dust, all of us the same thing.

My usual excuse for touring Nevşehir as to look at and maybe buy a couple of prayer rugs and some kilims, and here my interpreter, surely fifteen years my junior, took over and treated me like a toddler. While I sipped cup after cup of Turkish coffee, he haggled with the owner of whatever shop we were in until he got what he thought was a good price. Then he nodded, and off we would trot, my purchase rolled up and tied with twine. I liked the routine in a way, this giving myself over to a Big Daddy, but I was furious when he firmly forbade me to accept a dinner invitation for the two of us from the mayor of Nevşehir. I didn't have the right clothes (I had packed only corduroy pants and heavy sweaters); I would disgrace him. There was no way I could convince him that the mayor would forgive me my wardrobe, no way I could budge his stubborn Turkish stance. That evening, in an effort to make up for the toddler's disappointment, he took me to the weekly movie, where we sat on wooden benches and saw a double bill: a Turkish version of *The Wizard of Oz* and a costume drama, whose hero, he told me, was in jail more or less for life for possession of hashish. Every man, women, child, and infant in Nevşehir was at the movies that night, and when the voluptuous star of the costume drama, draped in roughly ten pounds of veiling, did a belly dance, the cheers were wild.

I liked him again then, liked him especially the next day, when we went through one of the underground cities, built perhaps by the Hittites, in a place called Kaymakli. Sometimes the ceilings were high enough for us to walk upright; more often we slid along on our bellies; in each instance our misery was mutual.

We emerged into a dusty, golden afternoon and the sight of a fat, bespectacled woman in a yashmak calling me to her house, the only one for miles and set in a sea of mud. Her name was Fatima; she had a son who was restringing a Moslem rosary and a husband kneeling on a prayer rug and facing Mecca. Neither acknowledged me while we sipped tea and talked in a language known only to women. True, we had no words but we had motherhood — she pointed to her son; I brought out a photograph of my daughters — and we had housekeeping. Her home had one room, whitewashed, carpeted with old pieces of linoleum, and lined with rug-covered banquettes, so there was little to tour but the walls. Pictures of Atatürk and Menderes, an executed premier, were pinned there, and postcards from tourists who, like me, had answered her wave. Somehow I made it clear that I had pictures on my wall, too, and together we mourned the difficulties of keeping a place clean and of raising children, and I don't know how we did this, but we did. Later, she pulled me outdoors, swathed me in a yashmak, pulled my arm around her shoulder, and the interpreter, who, bored by all this woman talk, had been waiting outside, photographed us with my Brownie Starmite. Because we were both veiled to our eyes, the only way one can tell which of us is the Turk and which is not is by my sweater. It came from the Aran Islands.

A few days later we drove to Konya, Turkey's holiest city, to the Mevlana Medresi, a museum and shrine to the thirteenth-century founder of the dervishes. Shoeless, I walked through kneeling, praying Moslems to see Mevlana's clothes and prayer rugs and Korans, the beard of the Prophet in an elaborate coffer, and Mevlana's tomb, hung with golden trappings. Then I, whose only God has been my father and, after his death, my husband, read what Mevlana said about being consumed with love for the God I could not find outside humanity. "I was raw," he wrote. "I am now cooked and burnt."

One of the small rugs I bought in Nevşehir disintegrated at the dry cleaners, and the other is stored in the basement. The kilims, I had made into pillows, and they are stored in a closet. A door knocker shaped like the hand of Fatima is stuck in the brick of my living room wall, and my blue worry beads disappeared a long time ago. So did a necklace with tiny blue stones and the presents I bought for the children. All but one. For Snow White I had bought a ring with the same tiny blue stones as were in my necklace, and it showed up not long ago, twisted now and tarnished. No matter how glorious one's children are in adulthood, it is painful to look at reminders of their childhood. The children who drank from those silver baby cups and carried those Flintstones lunchboxes will never again love as cleanly and as purely as they did then. Time will have darkened them.

"But what," you may ask, "happened to Snow White while you were in Turkey and she was at her father's country house?" I do not know. I suppose she went sledding and saw movies and, because she was getting interested in clothes, took to hanging around the area's quaint little shops. At night she probably popped popcorn and watched television, and, once put to bed, spent hours under the blankets reading by flashlight.

I do not know, however, what was going on in her head, or what it was that turned her into someone I had never before met. "Adolescents," a social worker told me once, "are walking time bombs."

I don't think I was. Neither was my sister. Or maybe we were and lacked only the fuse to set us off. But there were no fuses in a house in which two grandparents, two parents, and a maiden aunt built for us an armature that would last us all our lives. Perhaps those two weeks in the country marked the time that nature — can I call it nature? — stripped Snow White of those protections (I think of them as the immunities passed along in mother's milk) afforded by innocence. Oh, God, I am only speculating, fruitlessly as usual. Because if I, and all those parents who have seen their children turn into strangers overnight, knew the answers, we would no longer be asking ourselves — as we are always asking ourselves — "But what did I _do_?"

Five

Number 83 was beginning to fill up.
The Turkish rugs spilled color onto the bare floors, and two brown velvet couches arrived in the living room. "But Daddy's just bought the same couches!" the children said when the furniture was delivered. Having formed our tastes together, B and I, all unknowing, were constructing parallel universes. If they differed in any respect, it was probably in what we hung on our respective walls. During our marriage I had never entered an art gallery without him. Now I was hanging around Fifty-seventh Street, making choices that I knew would not have been his. Finally, I had broken with B's esthetic, and all it took was opening my mouth to say, "I'd like that collage, please," and a $25 deposit. The gallery owner would then root around in the coat closet for an old shopping bag, and off I would go to the bus, feeling like a Medici and clutching a purchase that, short of clothing, was the first in many years that was truly mine.

People started arriving, too. It was unnatural for someone who had once lugged copper pots and pans from Paris and cherished her few lessons with Julia Child's partners, Mmes. Bertholle and Beck, not to be feeding crowds, so I started inviting people for dinner and never gave a thought as to whether there was a man seated at the foot of the table, even though friends said an extra man made a useful bartender. I was proud of being able to handle anything short of a Manhattan — which nobody drank anyway, the only mixed drink I have ever known a New Yorker to like being a martini — and ran from ice cube tray to glass closet to the old wine carriers that held liquor bottles, feeling a power I had never known in marriage. Ceres I was, the great goddess, dispensing stuffed bass and a modest Sancerre as if I were reaping and sharing the fruits of the earth.

I was proud of everything I did on those evenings, rejecting the guests' offers to clear the table, bring out the dessert, make the coffee. Pride forbade my asking for help, pride and the fact, slowly dawning upon me, that I didn't need any. Perhaps I looked silly sometimes, hostessing, bartending, cooking, serving, and clearing simultaneously, but I never felt silly. Rather, I felt — as the guests murmured, "You did it again, Mary," and "Loved that chocolate mousse!" — the fabulous exhaustion of the long-distance runner. I had crossed the line. I had made it home.

I am a good cook and was turning into a pretty good talker, but I doubt that is why people came to the house. I think it was the house itself. Everyone wants to crawl into a cave once in a while, and although I have never had a place I thought big enough (wherever I have lived I have had the same dream, that of finding a previously unnoticed door and beyond it another room), I am a digger of caves. At night I would loose the living room curtains of their ties and pull them shut, turn on a few low lights and a little Lee Wylie, and then I, and everyone with me, was safe. Only in the rear, where there were no curtains at the big dining room window, did the house seem dangerous. If we were alone, the children and I ate our suppers as quickly as we could, fearful less of the intruder than of the impenetrable black out of which he might arrive.

Most of the neighbors had lived on the block for years. On summer nights they sat on their stoops, weaving tales out of the inconsequential, which are perhaps my favorite kind, because I can summon a profound interest in the possible reasons behind a favorite delivery boy's defection from one supermarket to another, or why the lights were on so late in So-and-So's apartment. It is the gift of growing up in a small town, I believe, this tendency to magnify the ordinary into the extraordinary. "Now tell me everything that happened," I still say to friends returned from holidays, "starting with when you got on the plane."

Once the weather became too cool for stoop-sitting, the neighbors disappeared indoors and issued last-minute invitations to come over for drinks. The women invariably wore long skirts, and one of the men invariably put on his sequin-striped party sweater, and all would greet one another with glad cries, even though they may have met at the supermarket a few hours earlier. I liked that; I like it when people put a sheen on their days. But I seldom sat on the stoops in summer, and I seldom went to the cocktail parties, because, a newcomer and diffident, I did not belong to the inner circle. "Mom," my younger daughter said sadly, as she watched people exchanging gossip from their respective front steps, "I don't think you're really a member of Jane Street society." She was right, but it didn't matter. What did matter was that on this odd, isolated block, I had an identity: the rather pretty woman at Number 83 who had two young daughters and a dog who was forever pulling frantically at his leash.

I also had an occupation distinct from my daily stint, one that imposed order on weekends which, *sans* church attendance, *sans* a husband carving the roast at Sunday dinner, _sans_ afternoon treats with Daddy while Mommy takes her nap, might otherwise have been made up of listless perusals of section after section of the endless Sunday _Times._ A few years earlier the then managing editor of _Mademoiselle,_ friend of the famous and giver of cocktail parties featuring skinny women and paunchy men who were always just back from or en route to Mount Desert or Hobe Sound, and who elbowed their way to the bartender with the ruthlessness of basketball players elbowing their way to the hoop, was looking for a food writer. When she listed the potential candidates, an editor whom I had fed often said, "I don't know why you're going outside for someone. You won't find anyone better than Mary."

For years I had wanted a chance to write something besides "a mere slip of a dress" or "damask carved like ivory," but I was too timid to ask, too much in awe of what I thought of as "real writers" and "real writing." Handed a modest food column, I was ecstatic, so much so that I never asked about money, which was just as well, because the managing editor wasn't planning to pay me any. So one Sunday every month, after having spent the previous weekends getting recipes from friends or little-known French magazines and testing them on the children, I would sit at my desk and lose myself in happy amateurism. The columns are, but for my adolescent occasional effusions, the closest thing I have to a diary, and among my favorite reading.

I do not like the view from my window today. It is a chilly Sunday and the air is gray, and for a week Con Ed has been tearing up the cobblestones so that the road in front of our house is one long trench railed with orange ropes. The few who walk by seem concussed, but no more so than our dog, Fred, who is asleep on the rug—flat on his back,

_paws dangling, and looking like a dead beetle. The three
cats and my younger daughter are staring mournfully at
this dismal landscape and I am staring mournfully at
a picture of myself taken when I was six. I have changed
for the worse . . ._

As I read that, the past sweeps over me, and my recall of
the pain that twisted my ribs whenever I thought of B
dissolves into images of the cats capering on my bed, of Rose
Red, wearing what she called her pancake hat, making Sunday breakfast, of Snow White, in love with Elizabeth I,
confiding stories of the Tudor court as if only she were privy
to them. If it weren't for those columns, pasted in a school-
child's three-subject notebook, I would have forgotten — so
powerful, maybe even preferable, is the memory of misery
— that there were many days at Number 83 when I was
joyous. When the balding man called to say he was coming to
town, I was excited, because now I was going to have the
kind of evening that society, by which I mean friends, psy-
chiatrists, and assorted magazines, said a woman of my age
and hormonal perfection should be having. Still, my feet
dragged when, babysitter installed, I left that paradise of
children, pets, and dinner on the stove to go uptown and pray
that the other people on the hotel elevator hadn't guessed
that the woman accompanying the man to his room on the
twelfth floor was not his wife.

Age — he was about ten years older than I — and alcohol
had taken its toll of the balding man, and although he
was never impotent, he was demanding. Neither the athlete
his publicity claimed nor the sexual Goliath his reputation
promised, he was more myth than male. That may not have
been true when he was young. "The first time I ever had a

girl, mah Mary, I couldn't wait and neither could she. So I took her on the kitchen table, only a room away from where her parents were sitting. Oh, mah Mary, I wish you'd known me then." But by the time we met he needed fantasy. I was Scheherazade.

Unless having read _The Story of O_ counts, I had only a nodding acquaintance with pornography. Once, a friend who was an incurable scavenger had picked up a pile of paperbacks from the floor of the office elevator ("The guys in the mailroom," she said darkly) and carted them to her apartment on a night we were dining together. While she was in the kitchen, cooking, I was in the living room, reading about a woman who preferred stallions, so hypnotized that I forgot my cigarette and it burned a small hole in her couch.

For the balding man, though, I became a teller of tales of Great Danes and girls' reform schools and female warders and whippings and frightened virgins on all fours, urged onward by his murmured "That's good, mah Mary, that's real good." Once I would have felt myself degraded by my nasty, nimble tongue, but not now. Telling stories to him so that he could make love didn't seem all that different from telling stories to my children so that they could sleep. "You don't need fantasy, do you?" he asked. "No," I said, "you're the fantasy," and snuggled along his magic back and slept.

Years later, marooned in someone's summer house, I picked up a copy of _The Pearl_ and laughed to see that I had the mind, and the limitations, of a Victorian pornographer.

Married, dishonest, drunk as often as he was sober, the balding man nonetheless added cubits to my stature when he came to the office. A certain contrived madness ran through its corridors; we hugged our craziness — "Women! We _are_ a silly race," the editor-in-chief was fond of saying — to our

Rudi Gernreiched bosoms. That I had to send my secretary out for a bottle of bourbon when he came in for a photo session, and that he once wrestled with a sturdy, knee-socked woman in the personnel department when she asked for identification from this unexpected caller, only added to my glory. True, I had not lost an entire skiffload of clothes while photographing on the Charles River, as had a fashion editor, nor did I keep a quart of Scotch in my bottom drawer, as was the custom with production editors. But I had a famous admirer, and so what if he sometimes seemed a sot? Wasn't that the price of genius? Wasn't I lucky to be partaking of it? My compliance — collusion, really — was predictable. I was, after all, the daughter of a man who believed that to be involved with books was to live at the heart of light, and the former wife of a man who shared his faith. Papa, however, had never met an honest-to-God writer, and B, who knew acres of them, was shrewd enough to separate the dancer from the dance. I was not.

When I semi-chaperoned *Mademoiselle*'s guest editors on their trips abroad, it was usually because they were going to a country the editor-in-chief didn't want to see. Who could blame her? Sad, raggedy Ireland suited me right down to the ground, but en route to Israel I nearly wept when we flew over the presumed glories that were Greece. I balked at Russia, too, despite knowing that I would never have such a chance again. But reluctant as I was to leave for Moscow, I was more reluctant to leave a house that was acting on me as an oyster does on grit. I knew what would happen, though, because it had happened before. I would be miserable for the first few days and ask myself, "Why did I do this?" Then, because travel was the only true cure I had for loneliness, I would sever all connections with my world and rock myself into the swing of a new one. I seldom sent postcards, and in Russia I didn't have the choice.

I remember little of Moscow, because I saw little of Moscow. Instead, I stood for hours at the Intourist desk in the hotel lobby watching while women thumbed through ledgers reminiscent of Bob Cratchit's, trying to confirm my travel plans. When I did go out, I was forever on the edge of the law, sitting down where I wasn't supposed to, suffering the warning whistles of policemen whose eyes were as opaque as pennies. The evening I finally left the city, I saw a box of matches on the airport floor, bent to pick it up (I was running out), then stiffened quickly, afraid of yet another shrill _nyet!_ No matter. The g.e.'s were well behind me, on their way back to New York, and I, armed only with a little Russian-English dictionary, was going to Uzbekistan and Siberia alone.

If you travel great distances in Russia, you are always flying at night and sliding in and out of time zones. All airport and official clocks were on Moscow time, maybe still are, so neither my watch, which I was doing my damnedest to set correctly, nor my body was ever in sync with the official hour. It would be an exaggeration to say that I hallucinated, but after a while time and space started shifting. I was there but I was not there. The sun was at this point but it was not. Conversations were sudden and absurd. Flying to Tashkent, I was so swathed in heat, I took off all the clothes possible as well as my shoes, and was sitting directly opposite an elderly, well-dressed American and his wife, both of whom were also barefoot. They were courteous people, and we exchanged a few courteous words about the godawfulness of Russian food before they fell asleep. A few hours later the man woke, smiled, looked down at my feet, which were planted a modest inch or two from his, and said, "I've always thought I could win any beautiful feet contest I entered, but I think you'd beat me." He dozed, and neither of us ever spoke to each other again.

Tashkent was where I shook to another whistle, because, exhausted from waiting eight hours in a torrid airport, I put my rope-soled espadrilles on a battered old coffee table, thus scarifying Soviet property. But it was also the place where, sick of the seedy lunchroom to which all foreigners were herded, I stubbornly stood in line at a rooftop Uzbek restaurant until a worn-down waitress finally sat me at a table full of Russian soldiers.

They gave me vodka, I gave them my American cigarettes, and together we talked and laughed about what, I cannot imagine, because we were communicating by semaphore and my little dictionary. But what a good time we had, and how well-companioned I was. My shishkebab was skewered horsemeat, and the champagne that came later, along with indecipherable toasts, was sickly sweet, but no matter. I was in the group, part of the party, not one of whose boisterous participants would have dreamed of daring me to down a glass of Scotch.

I hadn't danced for a long time, but now I was queen of the hotel's dollar bar, where I usually went after dinner for a coffee. Young Russians hung around there, in lieu of anywhere else to go, and all asked me to dance, thinking that I, an American, would know the new steps. I didn't, so I made them up, my shimmies and wiggles and windmill arms followed silently and intently by boys half my age. Then I would go up to my bed and pray for deliverance from a city where the temperature never dropped to bearable and the only cultural institution was a museum filled with photostats and replicas of Lenin's boyhood furniture. "Oh, God," I whimpered, "once I am out of here I promise I will never leave my children again."

Samarkand was different. It was just as hot, but here I could drag my mattress to the tiny balcony outside my room and listen all night to drums and clapping and the whine of Uzbek music. In the morning I rode the trolley out to the market, where all the fish were interred in one big block of dirty ice, climbed the hill on which the sextant of Ulugh Beg, a fifteen-century astronomer, had been excavated, and wandered through a park that was full of — is this possible? is my memory accurate? — Ping-Pong tables. In the afternoon I invariably visited the Shakh-y-Zinda, a complex of mosques, and the tomb of Tamerlane because they were close to the cherry-juice dispenser and the ice cream stand.

I never spoke unless it was to name my destination, except in the evening, when I shared my dinner table with a Canadian woman, a big-boned blonde with a raucous laugh, and an old Anglican minister from Bristol, England. When I told him I had grown up in Bristol, Rhode Island, he exclaimed, "Did you know Canon Parshley? Saint Michael's Church was so good to us during the war."

"He was one of my father's closest friends," I said excitedly, suddenly out of Samarkand, out of New York, too, and returned to what I persisted in calling "home." "My sister was a bridesmaid at his daughter Marjorie's wedding and . . ." There was no stopping my speech, not simply because once again I could use English, but because I could talk about a time before B, before children, before loss.

I had assumed the Canadian woman was much younger than I, since she giggled a lot about Russian officers met in the parks, and had glorious hangovers. Something of a snob, I had her figured for a secretary out on what my parents would have called "a toot," until the afternoon we were strolling along a street of mud houses and she started talking about herself.

She had never worked, never had to, only taken a course in flower-arranging at a famous London florist's. Like me, she had been married and divorced, but had given custody of her children, who were the same age as mine, to her husband. How could she be smiling and laughing and having such a good time when the end of her trip meant an empty house? I couldn't imagine living without my children, and panicked every time I thought they might be taken away. That fear was why I was so secretive about the balding man; why I lived a life so steeled with propriety.

After the Canadian woman left, the hotel dining room seemed very quiet, and the minister and I spoke often of her gaiety. "But I don't see," I said, "how she could have given up her children."

"I admire her courage," he said. "She believed her husband could give them a better home."

Disapproval had edged my voice when I spoke of the woman, and his charity shamed me. I had never thought about whether B or I could have given Snow White and Rose Red a better home. I thought only that I would die without them. Friends said I gave too much of my life to my daughters. The truth is that I would have had no life to give anyone were it not for them. What courage I had was for their sake: I had turned into a tiger the day Snow White was born. But without her and her sister to give me a reason for being, I might have been as flaccid, and as shapeless, as a jellyfish.

The minister's name is gone from my mind and he is probably gone from this earth, but I can still hear him telling me about his church's jumble sales and about the years he had saved money for this journey, so wild was he about

Islamic architecture, and how sad he was that he couldn't have saved enough for his wife to see it as well. I remember the nights he didn't come to the table, because, low on funds, he was eating alone in his room out of cans he'd brought from home. And I remember the morning when, soggy with tiredness, I met him at breakfast and he told me a ghost story.

"One night," he said, "I was home alone — my wife was visiting our daughter — and had gone to bed when I heard a knock at the kitchen door. I went downstairs, and there was a friend I hadn't seen in years.

"I let him in and led him to the kitchen. He was very hungry, so I fixed him a bowl of cereal and a cup of tea. He was also very tired — he said he'd had a long trip — so I showed him his room and went back to bed. The next morning he was gone, and I would have thought it a dream except that the cereal bowl and cup and saucer were still on the kitchen table. That night my wife called and said she'd heard he'd died two days earlier. Now Mary — may I call you Mary? — Mary, that is really true."

We were silent, I wondering if it had indeed been a dream, and hoping, because I longed for belief, that it had not been.

On the flight to Eastern Siberia the big string bag an old man had labored to bring on board the plane burst and sent dozens of oranges rolling down the aisles. The stewardesses had no interest in whether or not seatbelts were fastened at takeoff and landing, and passenger luggage was stowed in what seemed like hammocks over our heads. But by now I was used to Aeroflot; I was used to Russia; I was used to talking to myself. In Irkutsk, however, an Intourist guide (I had had none in Samarkand) suddenly appeared and took me to the churchyard where the Decembrists were buried ("This is a working church," I was assured) and on a hydrofoil across Lake Baikal and through street after street of elaborate wooden houses. "Why do you wish to photograph these?" she chided me. "They are old, no good."

She took me to a daycare center where all the children used their potties at the same time, and a woman gave me dolls for my own children. One evening I shared a restaurant table with a German engineer who, having asked me to write in my magazine about how much his countrymen wanted peace, made me feel like a Messenger to the World. Another day I was taken to tea with some middle-aged women who, laughing and excited, fussed with their hair and tugged at their girdles when I asked to take their picture. They gave me the best tea — oranges and sweet preserves to be eaten with little spoons — that Irkutsk could provide, and the hostess said, "I can hardly wait to tell my husband I had an American in my apartment." Suddenly I envied her the tiny bedroom with its brass bed, the tiny living room on whose couch her son slept, the tiny balcony on which she had placed pots of gloxinia. A husband came home at night and kept her warm, whereas I, resident of the land of the free and the home of the brave, and looking, though I was not, a generation younger than she and her friends, could not come in from the cold.

At night I lay in bed muttering my usual prayer — "Get me out of here and I will never leave my children again" — but when the time came, I was reluctant to leave Irkutsk. I had fallen in love with the old churchyard and the old Cossack houses and the little dachas out at Lake Baikal, and thought how fine it would be to stay here and write the town's history. A year or two ago I wanted the peace of the grave, and now I wanted the peace of the carrel and a burial in books. But I was kidding myself, I knew, not only because I had no Russian and had lost the habit of scholarship but because I had too little of what an Austrian friend called _sitzfleisch_, "sitting flesh." "You have no serenity," B had said more than once, and I didn't, not even when I slept. Out of waking life I would enter dreaming life, and emerge exhausted.

So I left on schedule, depending on my usual trick — following the people whose boarding cards were the same color as mine — to get me on the right plane. This time, though, there were no colors and I had to ask the members of an American tour group, pair after pair of Darby and Joans, if I was at the right gate. Without exception they drew back, averted their eyes, answered with nods, fearful of getting stuck with a woman traveling alone.

A few weeks before, on my first morning in Moscow, the three Russian men with whom I shared a breakast table offered me a drink from their carafe. I assumed it was mineral water. Instead, it was vodka, and they laughed, but not unkindly, at the look on my face when I took my first sip. Hearing I was from New York — they too had Russian-English dictionaries — they were dumbstruck. Had I seen the Empire State Building? Had I ever been to Radio City Music Hall?

The morning after my flight from Irkutsk I shared a breakfast table again, this time with an American salesman. "Why don't you stay for another day?" he suggested. "We could have some fun." Then he winked. So, in the morning sun, did his wedding ring.

To the Russians, male and female both, I had been a visitor from an almost unimaginable outside, treated with the kind of innocent curiosity that reminded me of the

questions — "Perhaps you have met my niece who is a waitress in a restaurant called Schrafft's in New York?" — that
country people had asked me on my first trip to Ireland a
long time ago. But to the Americans in the tour group, I was
that dangerous thing, a woman nearing middle age and on
the loose. To the American salesman, I was that easy thing, a
woman nearing middle age and on the loose.

A few hours later, taking a last walk through this city I
had never really seen, I strolled down a street lined with
linden trees just like those which had lined the sidewalk in
front of my high school. Their scent was, as always, heart-
breaking, and, just as the minister's mention of Canon Parshley had, brought me back "home." Then I realized at last
that all journeys — the final one, too, for all we know — are
circular.

Six

It was a warm autumn night in
New York, a few months after Moscow, too warm to sit in the
hotel lobby waiting for the balding man. So I crossed the
street and sat in Central Park, breathing in the green from
the trees that were still hanging on to their leaves and the
blue from gasoline fumes, glorying in being dressed up and
about to meet a man who, however ineligible, was someone I
could boast of knowing. I never did boast of knowing him,
though. I was afraid of B's hiring a private eye to find me an
unfit mother. "You ever see any guys in felt fedoras hanging
around?" my sister asked before my divorce. She, who had
liked him, and I, who had loved him, knew how I enraged B
simply by being myself. But, then, isn't that always the case
with husbands and wives, even when their marriages endure?

I looked east and there he was, my secret suitor, my
secret Santa maybe, coming up the street, carrying two big
Doubleday shopping bags. Wearing a leather jacket, his face
shadowed by a broad-brimmed hat, his shoulders bent forward by the weight of the bags, he looked like an aging
cowboy. Had he seen me first, he'd have raised his head and

started to strut, trying to belie the years that were written on his face and in the way his stomach had started to slide over his belt. But he didn't, so for once I saw him before he had a chance to put on his armor: slowed down by bags that had a weight he wouldn't have felt twenty years ago, and walking with an old man's flat-footed caution.

Usually we ate in his hotel dining room, but this night we went to a nearby restaurant. It was crowded, so we had to wait at the bar, and although people made room for us, no one looked at him.

"It's hard bein' a middle-aged man, mah Mary. If I sat on one side of a good-lookin' girl and some young truck-driver sat on the other, it wouldn't be me she'd turn to and smile at."

"Would that matter a lot?"

"Oh, yeah, it'd matter."

"You mean you want the applause of strangers?"

"Thass right." He laughed. "I like the way you put that. I want the applause of strangers. They're not out to get me, like my enemies are. But now Lowell is in the madhouse, and I am King of the Cats!"

"Mah Mary," he said later as he put down the telephone on which he had been talking to his wife, lying about his day and the way he was spending the evening, "I want you to understand exactly _who you are_. You are the other woman."

Bull. I am one of many other women and I know it. I say nothing, and he continues the performance.

"Now mah wife's a good woman, a good country gal, but . . ." I turn and look out the window, not because what he is saying hurts, but because he is pouring another bourbon, and the liquor, as they say, will start talking.

"Fat! She's got the sex appeal of a walrus. And squeamish! So _nice_ with that douche bag. She's always got a hose hangin' out of her."

I feel sick. I cannot bear the way he talks about his wife, but I sit silent because I am taking my punishment.

He is raging now and I am about to pick up my shoulder bag and leave, because God is telling me that my listening constitutes participation, that I am sinning again, when he shifts — he is always shifting — and says, "You want to hear a little guitar, mah Mary?"

He showed me her picture one day: she is dark and pretty with a nice straight nose. I think he loved her once, but even more incapable of surviving deep feeling than I, he had severed the nerve so that love was like a dead tooth in his head.

She telephoned me one New Year's Eve, his wife, when I was at a next-door neighbor's drinking eggnog. When I came home, Snow White, suspicion written all over her face, told me that while I was out a Mrs. —— had called. Surprised that his wife even knew of my existence, I waited all night for her to call again, fearing she would, fearing she would not. Because if she had asked me not to see her husband again, I would have said yes and meant it. I could not stop myself from seeing him. I wanted her to stop me.

Still, he sustained me for several years. I used to say good night to him, to the air, when I went to sleep, and I would always note the temperature in the city in which he lived when they gave it on the _Today_ show. I laughed through all our phone calls, while he played a harmonica and told shaggy-dog stories or we got excited about a book we were both reading. When he was in New York I sang to his guitar and capped his limericks, and we told each other stories about ourselves and our childhoods.

He was like an old shoe I couldn't slip off, and I was . . .
I don't know. One day he said, "Mah Mary, I think we're
kinder to each other than either of us has ever been to
anyone else."

He was lying supine and I was on top of him, as comfortable as if floating on a raft. My arms were folded across my
chest and over his and I kept nuzzling his lips open with my
mouth and kissing his tall, narrow teeth.

We always lay like that early in the morning, following a
familiar litany.

"You've got long teeth."

"My brother always said I should have got a dollar from
the tooth fairy when I lost one."

"You've got small ears. My grandmother says small ears
indicate stinginess or madness."

"Madness, mah Mary."

"Now that I see them in this light, I think your eyes are
more gray than blue."

"I always thought they were green."

"Never! Do you supppose you're a genius?"

"I suppose I am."

"But can I call you by your first name?"

"Sure."

"What'd you say your first name _was_, honey?"

He'd whoop and roll me off his chest, sit up, catch
me across his lap, and pretend to spank me. I'd wriggle,
never quite sure he wouldn't, and once, when I was twisting
around, I saw his face. It was puzzled. I think he was in love.

Who knows? Certainly not he. Was I in love? I've never
figured it out. All I am sure about is that I was grateful to
him for liking me. My husband did not. "I don't think he
could stand my silences" was the only answer I had when he
asked why B had left.

"Mah Mary!" he crowed. "Ah _love_ your silences."

Oh, I was grateful, all right, maybe even more grateful for the haven that was the hotel room. Because once I left it, I had to go home, and I couldn't bear what was going on at Number 83.

Lillian was dead. Early one morning I was sitting in my office, drinking coffee and reading the paper, when the phone rang. It was a friend. "Lillian died yesterday during an asthma attack, and someone found her late last night."

She had been alone, in her crazy-closet of an apartment, probably dressed in one of her trailing garments, the kind with the Mickey Mouse transfers, and maybe — I am imagining this part — grabbing desperately for her inhaler when she dropped. Snow White mustn't hear this, I thought, except from me, so I ran from the office and out into the street for a cab. When I am faced with death, my self-control deserts me, and Snow White, seeing my red eyes when I got home, knew something terrible had happened. I had no words but the simplest — "Lillian died yesterday" — and, looking hunted, Snow White turned and started to run up the stairs to her room.

I tried to hold her, but touch couldn't bring her back from the place where she was going. I begged her to come to church with me, but church meant little to her or her sister. I had been sloppy about Sunday school and religious instructions and lazy about Mass and resentful of every priest who had ever told me what to do even while I was silently begging to be told what to do. That Snow White couldn't have the consolation even of lighting a candle and saying a prayer for Lillian's soul — "Free her from purgatory," she could have said, "and bring her into heaven" — was my fault.

But I had that consolation. Nearby, on Fourteenth Street,

was a church built to hold a thousand or more parishioners and, now that the old Eighth Ward's old Irish had died out, empty most of the time. Tall and drafty and silent, smelling of floor wax and last Sunday's incense, it was just like the church I had known in childhood. I was that child again, shoving a dime in the slot, reaching for a spill, dipping it into a votive cup, and hoping against hope that my prayers were not just words lost in space. Then I came home, poured myself a stiff vodka, and sat crying in a corner of the living room.

The telephone kept ringing, friends of Lillian whom I had never met, and I spoke over and over again of getting her out of the morgue so that she could be buried from my house. The kind of funeral I was familiar with was preceded by a wake, and that was what I wanted for Lillian. I think she would have wanted it, too. But nothing could be done, so I cried some more and drank some more until Rose Red came home from school, determined as always to have a family like the one in *Little Women,* and frightened by my grief.

Still, there had been comfort in the lighting of the candle and the prayers, the merciful vodka and the tears I shared with those gulping strangers on the phone. Snow White, however, stayed in her room alone, without solace, and a long time later I found written on her wall, in green ink, "Lillian, why did you leave me?"

I took her to Dr. Franklin, and when I mentioned Lillian, I cried again. But Snow White was stony-faced and wouldn't talk about her. There was a second doctor to whom she went alone, but I heard from her father, whose suggestion he had been, that she wouldn't talk to him either. I think, though, that he was the doctor who suggested an institute that specialized in family therapy. When I told the man who was its head that the institute-supervised family weekend he recommended was a bad idea, he said, coldly, "Don't you want to help your child?"

Shamed into an alternative, I assembled, in the institute's formal living room, Snow White, her father and stepmother, Rose Red, who wept bitterly at her cruel distance from the life lived by Marmee, Meg, Jo, Beth, and Amy, and myself. This time I was the one who wouldn't talk. Instead, I reverted to the fearful child I had so often been with B and shrank in my chair. By now our marriage was something dimly remembered, or misremembered, but B had remained the only adult in the world whose approval I wanted.

Because the psychiatrist who presided over this torturous hour realized that family therapy was out of the question, she decided to see Snow White alone. During their hours together she fed her tea and cookies, and as long as Snow White was with her I could breathe again. But when, having made an appointment for myself, I asked what I could do, praying for guidelines and lists and modes of behavior, anything that would help me help my Snow White, the doctor said, "Just try being her mother."

As if I weren't trying! Snow White was living in a place I could not enter, no matter what my efforts, and I doubt that the doctor, smugly encased in credentials and self-confidence as she was, ever entered it either. But Lillian could. Somehow she could walk into Snow White's world and in it find ways to keep her moored to the middle class and its mores. Without Lillian and the giggles and jokes and whispers they shared, my daughter was beyond my reach or anyone else's.

One night, very late, when I was dozing I heard a knock at the door downstairs. The landlord had found one of the cats meowing in the front hall. I took the cat, went back to bed, and was slipping into sleep again when I remembered, with the kind of terror that keeps one mute in nightmares, that, hours earlier, when I had put the night lock on the front door, all the cats were inside. There was no way for one of them to have got out unless someone else had gone out.

I ran to Snow White's room. It was empty. Her bag was on the library table. She never went anywhere without her bag and its jumble of letters, diaries, and an address book of names only she would recognize, although many of their owners might not recognize her. They were people met in passing and perhaps never seen again. That she knew their names, however, made them, if only in her imagination, her friends.

I dialed B, so frightened that I could hardly talk. "You'd better search the cellar," he said.

Fred, the semi-Schnauzer, trailed me to the basement, and we searched together, the flashlight poking around the worn wing chair and tattered posters, and into the dark and dusty side rooms with their cargoes of paperbacks and 45s. But it was not them I was seeing. Instead, I saw all of Snow White's life, from the time she was a baby so beautiful I was afraid to hold and crush her, to the slouching mutiny she was now, eyes sliding, always sliding, walking with her pelvis thrust forward, more in threat than in invitation. I also saw all the times in between. Snow White slipping into sleep after the nightly reading of *Eloise*. The day when, her finger broken, she asked my permission before yelling "Shit!" as the doctor set it. The afternoon in Bristol when we sat on the rocks under the Mount Hope Bridge, trying to catch crabs with mussels tied on a string.

With the flashlight darting over the basement walls, I saw a hanging figure, sneakered feet projecting from a corner, a flaccid hand crowded with the silver rings she'd learned to make in a course at the YMCA. She and her father

89

had the same small, short-fingered hands, hands that made me tender because my own are so long and fierce. I saw the figure clearly, and then not at all. Fear had distorted my eyesight, made me see what wasn't there.

I came upstairs — it was two or three o'clock by now — and was dialing B again when I heard a key turn in the lock. I rebuked her; I told her she had frightened me, I told her it was dangerous out there. But mine was the impotent squawk of one who can no longer find words or voice or even passion. There was no way any longer to keep her off the dark streets and in the light of the house, so in the fall she went away to a boarding school in the Berkshires that B had heard of, for decades a kind of therapeutic _salon des refusés_ for the children of the literati, and now also a place to which the state of Massachusetts sent the occasional delinquent in lieu of juvenile hall. She kissed Fred and her sister goodbye, nodded to me, and left.

On Saturday nights when I walked up a nearby street toward the newsstand and the Sunday _Times,_ past a wire-fenced cement playground and its complement of teenagers giggling and groping in the dark, and, once, past a man in the doorway of a warehouse who, on seeing me, exposed himself, I would think of my elder daughter. She was safe now, in the country, and somebody else's responsibility. She was not out wandering through the city, in and out of a life about which I knew nothing, and I was not sitting up in bed waiting for the click of the lock downstairs, unable to look at her when she came in.

People say, "No matter what your pain, remember the child's pain is worse." I'm not sure. One is willing to die for one's child, and the hardest trial is that one is not allowed to do so. Dying is often easier than worrying, especially when the greatest worry is that one will stop worrying. Then one will die anyway, but of guilt, which murders slowly.

Parenthood, I realized, was a life sentence. My children could run away from home. I could not. My children were free to hate me. I was condemned to love them. When I was in the balding man's room, I was out on parole. With him, I was what I had been before I became barnacled with a husband, house, and children: a student, bookish, with a terrible crush on her teacher. I don't know what, during those dark strolls to the newsstand, I missed the most: the student, her teacher, or the room. No. I am lying to myself. I missed the man.

The winter Snow White was away, Rose Red's godmother died. We had met as college freshmen and as adults lived on adjoining streets. For many years we baked our Christmas fruitcakes together, she, a better baker than I, working the dough with her strong freckled hands while I greased the pans. The week before she died we were planning to have tea, but chemotherapy had tired her, and she forgot. A few days before Christmas, her house cleaned, her baking done, the presents wrapped, and the tree trimmed, she got into bed and went to sleep.

At her memorial service I sat far to the rear of the church, because I knew myself and my tears. I had tried hard to emulate my family's granitic stoicism, the calm and graceful faces they turned to the world when they were sick with sorrow, but the attempts were useless. When I got home the phone was ringing. It was the balding man, and he had no patience with my nose-blowing and my stuttering monologue. "What must be, must be," he kept saying. "You cannot fall apart like that."

But I can. When friends or family die, I leave a space for them, and not until that space closes of itself can I move on. If I try to rush the process with crowds and busyness, I am laying a thin sidewalk over a crevasse, and someday I will tumble in again.

A few days after the service I dreamed Rose Red's godmother came to the house, and together we went for a walk around the Village. As we walked she grew frailer and frailer and leaned into me so that I was half-supporting her, but we kept moving until two men arrived and picked her up, the size of a small child now, and carried her away on a silver tray. "It is funny," I wrote in a letter to Snow White, "but sometimes we say goodbye to people more finally in dreams than ever in real life."

"That dream you had," she said the next time I saw her, "that's the way I felt about Lillian."

"I wish you could see Bristol," I say to the balding man, who is sitting on the red couch at Number 83. It is the only time he has been here since the night we first slept together, four years earlier. Snow White is home from school for the weekend and is wary of him. But Rose Red, who would rather love than not, ran into his arms when he held them out to her.

Like a little girl who's brought home a new playmate, I am showing him all my treasures. We have been to my favorite Italian restaurant and he has liked his lunch, and since he is not an eater I am as pleased as a mother whose finicky baby has just finished every scrap. We have one of our favorite books, _The Journal of a Disappointed Man_, with us and I read aloud to him while we eat. The rest of the restaurant's customers are staring at us, but I am so used to his flamboyance and to concentrating on him, never mind

what people think, that I have at last lost the self-consciousness that made me miserable in public places.

We have reached the stage where, because we have been
together so seldom over the years, we keep bringing out and
brushing up the times we have been so that we can say,
"Remember when we were at the movies and you . . ." and
"Remember the night it rained and we were going . . ." thus
creating the illusion of a shared past. He has met the neighbors, about whom I had written him so much, and now we
are listening to "Dill Pickle Rag" on the stereo. We had been
in the garden, he picking burrs out of Fred's surprised eyebrows, I watching and wishing it would last forever: the
man and woman in the garden, the man playing with the
woman's dog, and a spring night coming down. He felt chilly,
however — he felt the cold more than I did — and we had
moved indoors.

We have been together for the last three days. As usual,
he has wanted me to believe that he is having nightmares
about World War II, and as usual I have put my arms around
him and said, "No, no, you're here with me now. Go to
sleep." It is a little game he plays, but he doesn't know I play
it, too.

As usual, we have had breakfast at the delicatessen near
his hotel, and as usual the owner, the man with the concentration camp number tattooed on his arm, has said, "Still
taking care of your girl, I see, Mr. ———." And he has said,
"Still takin' care."

We have sat at opposite ends of the big hotel bathtub,
unconscious of our nakedness, reading. First, though, I have
run the tub for him and shampooed his hair with a bar of
Ivory soap. He won't rinse the soap out — he says it makes
his hair look thicker — and later, immaculate, hair battened
with Ivory, he has gone to sit on a platform with a lot of

distinguished people while I sit in the front row wondering if, at the end of the speeches, I can leave by the family exit, the designated exit for the first three rows, since I am not family.

Behind me are assorted literati, all of them talking about grants and fellowships and applications to artists' colonies like Yaddo and MacDowell. Listening hard, I decide there is no angle they don't know how to work. Finally, as the ceremonial begins, they hush — all but the wife of a very famous writer, who is talking loudly to herself. Up on the stage Agnes Neel, who has just received a medal, is gesturing to the audience to applaud more! more! more! We laugh. An elderly critic, whose name is now more often in textbooks than in the newspapers, makes a speech about the Fugitive poets and sets everyone to yawning. A few more people get medals, and at last it is over. Daring the family exit, I walk outdoors and into a garden party, where the distinguished guests are attempting to mingle, although mingling does not appear to be among their talents. I think I am on Parnassus, and they know they are.

The balding man introduces me to a lot of people, and I am proud that I can introduce him to a lot of people. On the long cab ride back to his hotel, however, it happens, what I have seen happen so many times before. He is running down and, cold sober but exhausted, has put his head in my lap. I stroke the high, rounded forehead and the soap-stiffened hair and think to myself that if I die on the spot I'll be going out happy.

Tonight we are going to a dinner party, and I, tired of pretending to the children to be staying with a friend, have told them that I will not be home because I will be with him. Snow White is not surprised; she guessed long ago. At thirteen, however, Rose Red cannot bear to think of her mother being with a man. But I have told her that he makes me very happy and that I hope she can be happy for me. Too, Lucille, the babysitter who has kept us bemused for many years (once, when my daughters were ten and eight, she took them to a speech at City Hall, heckled the speaker, and landed the three of them at a police station), has told her, "Your mother is not an ordinary woman and you can't expect her to lead an ordinary life." I know I am a very ordinary woman, but Rose Red likes definitions and sliding things into their proper slots. Lucille has provided her with one for me. Also, she is an old-fashioned child, and, quite simply, she likes having a man around the house, if only for a short time. It makes her house more like other people's houses.

We go to the dinner party and in walks a woman with whom the balding man had had an affair. I think she is nice, and since the East Coast, not to mention the West Coast, is littered with his one-night stands, and I don't know much about his activities in the Midwest but assume he has maintained the same high standards, I am friendly and we chat. Later, though, she giggles and slides her eyes at him when we hear on the radio a song he always sings to me during my morning tub, one I thought was ours alone. Suddenly I am sixteen again, and my boyfriend has just stuck a knife in my ribs.

The balding man has started the evening booming and boisterous, but again he is running down. He is tired, too tired to eat, and if I don't leave with him right now, he hisses, embarrassing two guests who can hear him and not caring because he has a child's disregard of his tantrums, he is leaving with her, because "she always delivers." We leave.

He is quiet and I am angry, knowing that he is both a four-year-old who has had too much cake, ice cream, and excitement at the party and a grown man who has spoiled my golden day. I don't know which to speak to, so after he has crawled into bed I sit on the floor, leaning against the footboard, smoking and talking aloud to myself. "I don't know why you had to do that. I did nothing to provoke that attack. It was cruel. But what's worse is that I don't know why I left with you, why I'm here now."

He is quiet throughout the monologue, the cigarette, my later, stubborn silence. I move to the window embrasure and sit there, watching the headlights of cars driving through and past Central Park, turning to look around the room, at my clothes piled on the slipper chair, and the long mound on the bed. There is no air in this room — the windows cannot be opened — and I want very much to be out of it, out on the street, smelling the late spring that is wafting over the wall from Central Park and mixing with the curious meld of gasoline fumes and low-tide decay that is peculiarly Manhattan's. I love that scent because it is my city's scent, just as I love my city's rump-sprung taxis and the familiar bounce when they hit a pothole.

Oh, God, how much I want to be back in my clothes and out of this room and hailing a cab to take me home. I want to feel complete unto myself again. But I am not complete unto myself anymore. Something like an umbilical cord is connecting me to a man whose favorite jest is, "Well, I'll be a nigger aviator," and who, after once praising B, had said, "But I don't see how you could have done it."

"Done what?"

"Marry a _Jew._"

I am ashamed not of his speech — it is, after all, his sin — but of my silence. That, my moral cowardice, is the greatest sin. "Through my fault, through my fault," I am saying silently to myself, "through my most grievous fault."

The only sound is of the traffic fourteen stories below

the window, and I think he has passed out until I hear him say, "Maybe it's because you love me."

I get up then and slip into bed beside him. Both of us are speechless and stiff as effigies. "I feel so alone," I say at last. "So do I," he says. We turn to each other and he drifts into the serene sleep of those who can, and always will, get away with murder.

Seven

Once, when I was still married,
I had a strep throat and, thinking it cured, stopped taking my
penicillin. A day or two later I found nodes on my shinbones,
was sent by a nervous dermatologist to a heart specialist, and
was told I had something called erythema nodosum. I had
never heard of it before, have never heard of it since, and
perhaps I have the wrong words for it. All I know about the
ailment is that it can indicate rheumatic fever, nephritis, or,
as in my case, the foolishness of cutting back on one's penicillin.

For several weeks I stayed in bed, because walking was
close to impossible, while Rose Red, too young for school,
sat on the floor beside me and played her toy xylophone.
She had also arranged what she called a "comfort table" —
one of a stack of TV tables, draped with a dishtowel and
equipped with a glass, a comb, and a book chosen at random
because she couldn't read — and put it within easy reach.
Despite the pain in my legs, I had never been so happy.

While our Jamaican nurse, Hoppy, fetched Snow White
from nursery school, Rose Red napped on my chaise longue,
and when her sister got home neither could bear to leave the
bedroom because, for once, they had me to themselves. To

this day, I am saddened by the speed of Rose Red's speech. Talking fast, she figured, was the only way she could cram what she wanted so much to tell me in the little time I had to listen.

But now, the office being out of the question, there was time to hear about what Snow White had cooked on the toy stove at nursery school and where Rose Red had gone on her morning walk with Hoppy. There was time to hear them chattering downstairs while Hoppy gave them their baths, time to listen to Lucy and Desi, although I was too far away to hear anything but Desi's occasional "Looo-cy!" Illness had sentenced me to a term as their mother and my husband's wife, and I loved my prison.

Early evenings were the only part of the day in which I was alone, and then I would put down my book and turn toward the bedroom window, to watch the dog in the window of a red brick building across the street. The dog was a small white poodle, and along about five o'clock, it would climb onto the sill, wriggle itself in front of the Venetian blind, and stare up the street toward Eighth Avenue. Twenty or so minutes later it would commence a barking that, of course, I couldn't hear, then wriggle past the blinds again to jump from the sill. A minute or two later a light would go on behind the blind; a woman whom I could see only in silhouette would raise it and vanish into what must have been the kitchen.

The kitchen was beyond my sight, but the table at which she sat was not. Every night I noticed the care with which she set it for her solitary meal and invariably lit a pair of candles. I admired that woman, whose face I never saw and whom I could not have recognized had I passed her on the street. Left to dine alone, I would probably live on ends of salami and sardines on crackers. But I didn't have to dine alone; I would never have to dine alone. B would be with me, as he was about an hour later, sitting on the chaise longue and telling me about his day. Like the children, he too wallowed in my undivided attention. "I like to play with my mind," I had once told Dr. Franklin in explanation of the captiousness of my attention span. "No, Mees Cantwell," he said. (His Mitteleuropa accent was as adhesive as Krazy Glue.) "Your mind likes to play with you."

For years thereafter I was never again physically sick, although during the time beween B's leaving and our divorce I prayed for pain, for an illness that would hurt so much that it would erase the illness in my head. It didn't come. Often I longed to faint, to be deaf and blind and unknowing. But the heart pumped, the blood traveled, the engine drove without a stutter. Eventually, I learned to love my body, the way my fingernails, drawn lightly across the skin, could erase an itch and the way the bone seemed to rise to meet the palm I laid on my cheek. My legs could cover miles of ground with the regularity of an automaton's; my hair grew without orders. How could anyone wish to transcend the body? Three score and ten was far too short a time to explore the cosmos bounded by my skin, and eternity a terrifying word. But one Saturday in June the engine finally faltered.

My head had ached for three days, but that was nothing new to a veteran of migraine. By Friday night, though, I had a fever that left me dry and burning one minute, cold and wet the next.

My sole doctor was my obstetrician, and he was away. So was Rose Red's pediatrician, the only other doctor we could think of. The doctor suggested by a neighbor was away, too. The children called Lucille, who knew everything, and she suggested a medical student who lived nearby and who might have reached a chapter in his studies that covered whatever I had, and a chiropractor who was a faith healer and who worked through the feet. Eventually Rose Red telephoned for a cab — the taxi services were just beginning to make house calls — but when the dispatcher heard the destination, St. Vincent's Hospital, he sent no one. Maybe he feared a birth in the back seat of the car or, worse, a demise.

At last I got out of bed, and, wearing a bra, underpants, a wrinkled green caftan, and Dr. Scholl health sandals, carrying a bag with a lipstick, a hairbrush, and my Blue Cross–Blue Shield card, I walked through the Village's steamy streets to St. Vincent's emergency room.

There I lay for a long time on a cot in a cubicle while my sweat soaked the mattress, listening to a young girl on the other side of the curtain who'd come in with a venereal disease. She had a sweet, soft voice and seemed shy, and she cried and moaned as a doctor, who spoke gently and kindly, cleaned out her vagina. And I, with little else to think of, thought of how the body declares a moratorium on sex, how the body itself proscribes promiscuity.

I lost track of time and didn't know that the children, teenagers now and nervous because I hadn't returned home, were sitting in the lobby outside the emergency room. A nurse pulled the green caftan over my head, pausing to ask, "Is this a Carol Horn?" referring to a designer of medium-priced sportswear, before tossing it into a garbage bag along with the underwear and the Dr. Scholls. Then she tied me into a hospital gown and called an orderly, who wheeled me out of the emergency room and through the lobby. Dripping wet, whiter than the sheets, a garbage bag holding my clothes and purse plopped by my right hand, I lacked only a tag on my big toe to proclaim me a corpse. Tired, I closed my eyes, and a moment later opened them to see a muddled, almost incredulous Snow White standing beside the gurney. "You can come and see your mother in a few minutes," the orderly said.

St. Vincent's is a Catholic hospital, and someone had left a piece of a Palm Sunday palm draped over the crucifix on the wall of my room. Seeing it, I released myself . . . to God or fate, I guess. They are the only words I have to describe that letting go of my self. Snow White was with me and so was that crucifix and I didn't need anything else, not even the priest who arrived a few minutes later. But I needed the nurse's aide — plump and black and glossy as a plum in her pink uniform — who threw herself across me while a doctor did a spinal tap. Without her sweet, solid flesh to pin me into place, I might have moved, and the needle, of which I was afraid, might have wandered. "Thank you, God," I breathed, thinking her an angel.

As the days passed and I realized that I must be very sick, I called a friend and said she'd better tell B. Everything and everyone else fell away. Always a conscientious housewife, I finally had my house in order. The bills were paid, my will was made, and my children were strong and straight. As for the balding man, I knew that I would take on more reality dead than fleshed. He had buried a lot of women, or so he claimed, and he had loved them all, more in death than in life. I would become one of his gallery of dearly beloveds. Besides, I would not really die, because every day those two mock-ups of myself — Rose Red stiff-backed and determinedly tearless, Snow White anxious to get on with her constant circling of the Village and its lures but there nonetheless — were standing on either side of my bed, not me, but me, and living. At last I had a free pass to the Father, by whom I really meant Papa, and I was going with a collection of venial sins but no mortal ones. My duty was done, and the last thing I would see with earth's eyes was my daughters, my descendants, growing like trees.

Rocky Mountain fever, or a version thereof (no one was ever really sure), was diagnosed. I was dosed with Tetracycline, and my world expanded to include the morning papers being pulled past my room on a little red wagon and the old woman in the next bed who, half-dead from emphysema, hid cigarettes in her Kleenex box and crept from the room, when the nurses weren't looking, to smoke on the fire escape. Our room was opposite the back door to the kitchen, and when at night I saw a few ambulatory patients lined up for leftovers, I told a nurse I was starving, and she sneaked me a slice of chocolate cake and, in lieu of a fork, a tongue depressor. A neighbor came over with my typewriter; a friend brought pounds of cherries into which my hand dipped with metronomic regularity.

Still, I missed those days in which I had floated, only my nose poking from the water, and those nights of thermometer-interrupted sleep. I missed cotton blankets that absorbed sweat and rubber gloves filled with ice cubes and laid along my groin while nurses whispered. One seldom gets to die before the final death, to have the final view and live to look again, to see what is extraneous and what is not. In the end I saw my children, and nothing else. Now it is hard to remember that, just as now it is hard to reconstruct pain or love, time being a kind of universal solvent, but I want to remember. Because I read *The Waste Land* during my first year in college, it has sunk into my skeleton, and whenever I think of "these fragments I have shored against my ruins," I think of what to me will always be "my girls."

One of my girls, though, was leaving home again, not for the boarding school in the Berkshires this time but for a place on

Eighth Street. From her former classmates, she had acquired the skills of a jailhouse lawyer and was now, she told me, a "self-emancipated minor." It was on a late November afternoon she left, carrying shopping bags crammed with clothes and the dented pots and pans she'd saved from trashcans for a kitchen of her own. Now there would be no mother to say, "Where have you been?" and "Where are you going?" and no sister, busy with her homework, begging her to turn down Janis Joplin. Now there would be another school, this one, too, stocked with misfits but not, thank God, with juvenile delinquents, and other friends whom probably I would never see or, if I did, learn to like.

The shopping bags were draped over her left arm. Tucked under her right was one of the Hallowe'en pumpkins I had carved for her and her sister. "You're still a child," I longed to say when I saw it. But she wouldn't have believed me, nor paused for a second in her dogged walk toward an adulthood she construed as freedom from all adults.

Whenever we parted the balding man would say, "Mah Mary, let me lay this on you. If we ever *could* marry, and I'm not sayin' we ever could, would you marry me?" I always said yes. "I'd come to you in my shift," I would say, in love with the sentence, which I had read in a book or heard in a movie, and safe in saying it because I knew I would never be put to the test.

One morning, in bed with his arm around me, he said, "Oh, mah Mary, we're never going to be able to get married."

"I know that, but we have to believe we can."

"Think you could manage in an academic community?"

"Of course."

"Bet you're a good hostess."

"Yup."

"Can you run an adding machine? Mah wife can. You ought to see her fingers fly. I'm practically a conglomerate, y'know."

"No," I said, "but I can hire someone who can."

I was lying. I could run an adding machine. But there were limits beyond which I was not willing to take this conversation, and a possible career as an accountant was one of those limits.

He could be as blunt as a hammer, and as destructive. "The only person I'd marry if I didn't marry you would be some idealistic twenty-one-year-old I could train and teach and . . ." My eyes reddened, and the balding man added quickly, "Now, mah Mary, don't get upset about a rival you haven't even got."

I never thought of his wife as a rival. I never, away from him, fantasized a possible marriage. What he gave me, or, rather, what I took from him, was our shared passion for language, which may not seem like much compared to a marriage and children and the way B had looked at me on our wedding night. But it was all I wanted, especially since it came from someone whose work I loved. Had he been a lesser writer, he would have been a lesser lover. No, I am lying. He would not have been my lover at all. I could overlook a lot of imperfections, but not a rotten prose style.

Sometimes I thanked Jesus for the balding man, believing that he represented absolution. If earning that absolution meant enduring indignities, it was the price I had to pay for having heaped indignities on B — for not having been a good wife — and on my children — for my failure to make a home in which their father could be happy. Waiting, frightened, in a hotel room for a house detective to burst through the door and haul me away for prostitution, knowing that every lie I told my daughters about where I'd spent the night meant a black mark on the white paper that was my immortal soul, knowing the mark was even blacker when, by my silence, I conspired in the balding man's bigotry: these constituted my punishment.

Once, we fought, and when I accused him of lying to me, he said, "Yes, I lied. But what has truth to do with me? I'm an artist. I _make_ the truth," and I, impatient with so artsy-fartsy a distinction, had gone home. As I walked in the door, the phone was ringing. It was he, and he was crying. "Mah Mary," he said, "we mustn't lose this."

I was crying, too. We'd come too close to severing the cord that connected us. Occasionally the cord had had to stretch five thousand miles or six months, but it never broke. I knew other men. One proposed and a second hinted, but I was already married, to him, and I would have been happy to stay married to him for the rest of my life. I suspect, too, he might have been happy to stay my make-believe husband for the rest of his. But reality got in the way.

Early one autumn morning he phoned and said his wife was dying. Would I marry him? At first I was stunned. I had never wished her dead. I had never wished anyone dead except, when the night's zero hour and mine coincided, myself. Then I remembered another morning, several years ago, when he, fond of drama and of playing wolf, had called to say that his wife was very possibly breathing her last. That time I had cried for hours, thinking myself — with the guilt-ridden's arrogant belief in her power — partly to blame. So this time, wary of his playacting and the pleasure he took in turning circumstance into crisis, I said something vague about how he should think only of her and not of any future we might have together, because I had always been with him and I always would be. That afternoon I told a friend he'd probably been on the phone all day proposing to everyone in his address book.

In a week she was indeed dead. A week after the funeral he called me. Two days later he came to New York.

A few nights before he arrived I was standing at the bedroom window looking out at the street, which was wet and empty. A woman appeared, walking toward the docks, drunk and waving an umbrella at nothing. There was a time when I would have felt sorry for her, poor soul with no roof over her head. This time I thought, "Maybe she likes it outside, and yelling." Maybe I did, too.

True, I had a roof over my head. I had raised it myself, and there is no pride like the pride that comes from being able to build a house for oneself. But for six years I had lived outside the world where the animals went into the ark two by two. It was a world I had lived in for a long time and since I was very young, and although I was ambivalent about moving back in, not marrying the balding man would have meant losing him. Or, to be more precise, losing the only strong connection I had ever made to any man besides my father and B.

We were to meet at the delicatessen where we always had breakfast. He was late, so I stood outside in the morning cold, my eyes fixed on Sixth Avenue and the corner around which he would appear. A woman I worked with came by, walking her dog, and asked what on earth I was doing fifty blocks from home at nine in the morning.

"I'm having breakfast with an old friend," I told her. "If you see my secretary, tell her I'll be in a little late." I spoke calmly, but my body was urging her to walk on so that I could be alone when I saw him. The dog pulled on its leash, she waved a casual goodbye, and moved toward Fifth Avenue just as he rounded the corner of Sixth, wearing his big hat, his hands stuck in the pockets of his bulky sheepskin jacket. I ran to him, slid my arms inside the jacket and around his waist, and laid my head on his chest for a moment. We walked slowly, my right arm still around his waist, to the delicatessen.

I carried my coffee to a table, and we sat facing each other.

"Thank you for that lovely letter, mah Mary," he said of my condolence note. "Of course I know you only wrote it because you want to marry me."

The floor opened and the walls slid away and I was dizzy. There was nothing to hold on to but that cup, so I wrapped both hands about it and stared. His eyes were those of a breeder at a horse auction.

"Tell me about your daughter. I've got to know everything about her if you're going to be mah wife."

I told him about Snow White, but not everything about Snow White. My child was entitled to her grief, her terror, and, above all, her privacy. "But she's got a good pyschiatrist, whom she likes," I finished, "and she's coming out of it."

"Mah Mary," he said, "there's somethin' awful wrong here. A child who hates her mother. And I just don't think I can take on your financial responsibilities."

I was enraged. How dare he imply that I couldn't provide for my daughter, or that her father, that "Jew," would not?

"If you don't want to marry me, don't," I said. "But don't you dare use my children as an excuse."

He asked a few more questions. He did everything but check my wind.

"What is this?" I asked. "A job interview?"

"What do you think it is?"

"A job interview."

He walked me to the corner and I got in a cab. A glass

bell had dropped, the bell that drops whenever air might crumble me, and I saw Fifth Avenue, and later my desk, my secretary, the magazine's "staffers" walking past my door, from the inside looking out. I didn't cry and I didn't faint. I was as sealed in, and as dead, as the stuffed canary under its dome on the library mantel. That night I went with an old friend to a party for the balding man. Together we watched the performance: the smiles, the hugs, the swelling of the corpse. "Are you sure you want that, Mary?" my friend asked as he took me home. He didn't say "him." "Him" had disappeared.

I had tried to keep my father from dying; I had tried to keep my husband from leaving; I was equally incapable of letting the balding man go. We had dinner the next evening. When he cried about his wife and about watering the plants himself, I cried, too, because I couldn't bear the image of him with a little brass watering can in his hand.

Sometimes, though, his martinis and the novelty of his new role dried his tears, and then he was as giddy as Pandora facing the box. "You wouldn't believe the number of women willin' to console the grievin' widower. You know ———?" (He named a well-known novelist, someone who, because I was still too naïve to realize that a widower's phone starts ringing about ten minutes after his wife's interment, I thought beyond pursuing the bereaved.) "She called last week."

Then he spoke again of his wife, swinging as ever between love and anger, and I cried some more, for both of them. We soaked the restaurant's pink napkins with our tears, and when my handkerchief, which we'd been sharing, was soggy, we blew our noses on them. I don't know if anyone noticed us. My eyes were on him.

We went to his room. We were calmer now, and we started talking about a "decent interval" and an Irish writer we knew. He asked if I would like to go to Ireland again "with your husband."

"Oh, yes," I said. "We'll go to the Dingle Peninsula. Have you ever been there? We'll . . ."

I was sitting in a club chair, my hands open on my lap, my stocking feet crossed on the bed, feeling the familiar ease fall over me. He brought out his guitar. "Let's make up a blues," he said.

"She's a New York woman," he sang, "and she's got big brown eyes. She's a New York woman . . ."

"And she's tryin' me on for size."

He laughed and hugged me. "Mah Mary. We are _fated_ to be man and wife."

He wanted me to spend the night.

"But I can't. I would have called a sitter to come and stay overnight, but you said you were leaving terribly early in the morning, so I didn't think . . ." I didn't add that, with his wife a few weeks dead, I thought he'd want to give her her space in his bed just a little longer.

"Your daughter is old enough to stay alone."

"No, she isn't," I said, thinking of New York and open windows and a figure sliding noiselessly under the sash. "She'd get scared."

"Mary, how can I marry a woman who can't manage her time?"

"That's not fair. I manage my time very well. I . . . come on. You get into bed and I'll read you to sleep."

He undressed and lay down, curled on his side. I pulled a sheet over him and sat in the crook of his body and read sections of one of his own books.

"Young man who wrote that's got a pretty big future," he said.

"He sure has," I said.

"Man who wrote that hasn't done *half* of what he's goin' to do."

"I know. Remember that time at Lincoln Center when that boy waited in the dark to tell you how much he admired you, and I said, 'Doesn't that make up for everything?' and you said 'No.'"

"I was lyin', mah Mary. It makes up for a lot."

We were silent for a moment, and I pulled myself higher on the headboard.

"Y'know. I was a good-lookin' boy in my youth."

"I know that, too. I can still see him."

"I keep thinkin', mah Mary" — and he rolled over on his back — "that if I get back into trainin', I could be an Olympic runner even now."

"I'm sure you could."

I wasn't humoring him. I had always believed he could do anything but love anyone very much.

"Mah Mary, thank you. You can't imagine what these last six weeks have been like. You've restored me."

He was sleepy now, so I got up and turned off the light.

"Mah Mary," he said in the dark, "I want you to make me a statement. *Do you love me?*"

"I love you very much."

"Would it hurt you a lot if we didn't marry?"

"Yes," I said, "it would hurt me a lot."

Four weeks later he married a student. "She restored me," he told the press.

I was saving the morning paper to read with breakfast, so I didn't know until someone called and read the little news item aloud. Speechless, I hung up the phone, left the kitchen, went into the bathroom, and turned on the shower. I was so cold my bones felt iced, so I stood for a long time in the stream of hot water, but they didn't melt.

I left the house and walked, I always try to walk off sadness, heading crosstown to a friend on Fifth Avenue. "Age," she said, "his age."

Punctilious as ever, I walked to a Christopher Street hairdresser's to keep my appointment. After my shampoo, while I was waiting for the haircut, I went to the pay phone on the wall and called the friend who had asked me if I was sure I wanted "that."

"Leo," I said, starting to cry, "he blew it."

"You had too much baggage," he said.

Dr. Franklin, whom I had not seen for a long time, found an hour for me that afternoon. He had seen me cry till my tears wet my skirt when B left, and once again he was looking at me, bent over, trying to stanch my running nose.

"Mary," he said, for once breaking through the formality that had been our style for many years, "you have a tendency to fantasize."

"Did I fantastize those years? Those proposals? Last month?"

"No. You fantasized the man."

Soon after I got home, the doorbell rang. Two friends, a man and his wife, had driven in from Long Island when they saw the paper. By now my eyes were slits and my face was swollen. I couldn't cry enough. It was like the time many years ago when I had had food poisoning and vomited until I was heaving only air.

"I don't know why, but I keep remembering the afternoon my father died," I said as they came in. "His bed was in the bay window of the living room so that he could watch people going by, and we were all standing beside it when his breathing got heavy and he went into a coma.

"I said 'Papa!' and the nurse, a family friend, said, 'Mary Lee, don't. It makes it harder for them to leave if they hear somebody trying to call them back. Let him go.'

"When his breathing got even heavier, she ordered us into the dining room, because he had told her he didn't want any of us to see him die, not even my mother. We sat there until we heard the breathing stop.

"You know what? He's been dead so long now I can't even remember his face. But I keep looking at the door," and I pointed toward the hall, "because all I really want is for it to open and my father to walk in."

After they left, I splashed my face with cold water until it was scarlet and put cold tea bags on my eyes so that Snow White, who had been spending the Christmas holidays with us, and Rose Red wouldn't see that I'd been crying when they came home from calling on their father. The tree was still up, and I sat next to it, breathing in the balsam. Minutes passed, and as they did, something funny started happening to my back. It was as if a pack were sliding from my shoulders, leaving me lighter by ten pounds. I have paid the penance for failing my husband, I told myself. I have been absolved. I felt as I did on the Saturday afternoons of my childhood when, my soul as clean as unmarked paper, I left the confessional and walked as if on zephyrs across Bristol Common toward home.

Eight

On my way to Australia five years earlier, I had stopped overnight in Honolulu. As I got off the plane, a fat woman in a muumuu draped a lei over my head and handed me a bottle of a local firm's suntan lotion. The fashion editor, the photographer, the enormous box, always called "the coffin," in which were packed the clothes to be photographed, and I were then driven to a hotel on a high-way that might as well have been the New Jersey Turnpike. At sunset a series of drumbeats, on tape, was played over the lobby's public address system while torches were lighted around the hotel swimming pool.

I had a drink served in a coconut shell under the thatched hut that was the outdoor bar, and drove with the editor and the photographer, *sans* coffin, to a fern-thicketed restaurant, where we ate tinned shrimp in a gelatinous sauce over instant rice.

The next morning I looked for the Pacific. Wearing a swimsuit and carrying the suntan lotion, I picked my way along the edges of countless swimming pools until I found a gritty track that led to a lagoon. It was not quite the Pacific; it was as tepid as a tub drawn and forgotten. But it was the best I could do.

Now, a few years later, I was back in Hawaii, on an island called Lanai, just a hop and cheap ticket away from the small northern California town where I had been describing the life, times, and makeup mistakes of a group of young women who had written *Mademoiselle* asking to be "made over."

We — a beauty editor, a hairdresser, and a makeup expert — stayed in an old hotel outside of which was a plaque screwed to a rock celebrating the generous ladies who, during the Silver Rush, had made the days and (mostly) the nights bearable for prospectors and lumberjacks. The bar across the street had customers by seven in the morning, the sidewalks were wooden, and the air was pure as Eden's. By day, while I took notes, the traveling troupe cut hair, brushed on blush, and introduced the novitiates to the miracle that was the eyelash curler. At night, we all dined together, so linked in comradeship and our sense of a superior esthetic — "Did you see the one with the purple eyeshadow and the awful shag?" — that we strangers seemed old friends and this town, our town, Once the job was over, however, we were over, too. Everyone went back to his or her real life, all but me, who was grateful for the hiatus that would delay the return to mine.

Lanai, which was tiny, produced pineapples but no palms, had a tall lava shelf but no cliffs, a string of sand but no sweep of beach. I've been twice to Hawaii, but since I've never seen any of its geographic wonders, never even been to a luau or watched a hula, one could say I've never been there at all.

Running, of course. I ran to a man. I have done that more often than I have acknowledged to myself. But I do not see men as amalgams of muscles, penises, and hair in places in which I have none. Rather, they are enormous easy chairs in which I like to sit a while. Frederick Exley, though, was nobody's idea of an easy chair. It was just that over the years during which he had visited Lanai, staying with his childhood friend Jo and Jo's wife, Phyllis, once a nightclub singer in the Philippines, he had handed out invitations thick and fast, serene in the conviction that nobody was ever going to show up. I fooled him.

Lanai was mostly flat, with a bony spine called the Ridge running through its center, and was notable mostly because it was *not* flat and was home to some rare insects. Seldom has a developer had less to work with, but the island has since become chic, thus fulfilling Fred's worst fears. Money did it, of course, and Fred, while deriding the rich, would have liked a stab at being one of them. But not as much as he would have liked to walk down Fifth Avenue and hear people murmur, "That's Frederick Exley, the famous novelist."

"Other men," Fred wrote of himself, "might inherit from their fathers a head for figures, a gold pocket watch all encrusted with the oxidized green of age, or an eternally astonished expression; from mine I acquired this need to have my name whispered in reverential tones." Because of that need, I have eschewed my customary discretion (memoirs, after all, are never the whole truth, only that portion their authors choose to discuss) and revealed his name. Were he still on this earth, he would have killed me if I hadn't — not by the sword but by a torrent of speech, which, when Fred was in full form, could fell an ox.

I treasured Fred's first book, *A Fan's Notes,* and never argued when he claimed his second, *Pages from a Cold Island,* was better. It is hard for a writer who longed, as he put it, to produce "a shelf" to admit that he may have done his best work on his first time out. The two novels that followed, and a few occasional pieces, were postscripts.

A stocky, bearded man in his late forties, Exley had

considerably more gut than when I first saw him, a few years previously. He wasn't writing much on Lanai. He was "circling," he said. In the evening, when he put on his seersucker pajamas ("Like my 'jammies, Mary?") and his big straw hat, slathered a plate with Pecan Dandy ice cream, climbed on the couch, arranged an afghan over his feet, slid his vokda bottle, which lacked only a nipple, within easy reach of his right hand, and talked back to the television set, he was our child. Jo and Phyllis's children by their former marriages were grown and far away, and I am a mother before I am anything else, so we all needed a baby.

Fred and I met when I went to upstate New York, to Alexandria Bay, where he had a small, pin-neat apartment in a gangling Victorian house. *Mademoiselle*, like every other magazine that year, was celebrating the two-hundredth anniversary of the Spirit of '76, and I, who thought him the quintessential male American writer, wanted him in the issue. Fred, though, didn't know or care why I'd flown upstate in a little plane that at one point seemed to brush the treetops. All he wanted was his picture in the papers.

We shook hands shyly and got into the car he'd borrowed from a "buddy" — all Fred's friends were "buddies," and I doubt he'd ever had enough money for a car of his own. Before I had settled myself in the seat, he said, "All I know about you is that you're B's ex-wife."

"Do you know him?"

"No. But when I finished my first novel somebody said I should have an agent. So I sent it to him. He kept it for what seemed a verry long time, and when I called him about it, he said he didn't want to handle the book, then added some verry gra-too-i-tous ree-marks. When it won all those awards, I felt like calling him again and saying, 'Fuck you, B.'"

"Dear Lord," I thought, "what a start for an interview."

I needn't have worried. Fred liked to talk. It wasn't long before he forgot my ex-wifehood, and only a little longer before he forgot my sex. He was describing how, when in college and penniless, he was persuaded by a friend to service a homosexual who paid well.

"But, Cantwell, I just couldn't do it. You know how it is when you've been swimming and you come out of the water and your prick is cold and limp?"

"No," I said.

His ears blocked by the sound of his own voice, he didn't even laugh.

Interviewing creates a spurious intimacy. If one is a good interviewer and the interviewee is a willing talker, the two of you become, for several hours, each other's best friend. When the interview is over, so is the friendship.

Fred was an exception. A lonely man, he was not comfortable face to face with most women — he preferred them groin to groin and gone before breakfast — so the phone became an intermediary. His vocabulary was that of the best man at a prenuptial smoker, and he never failed to make me laugh.

"Cantwell," he would growl over long distance, "there's this cunt up here . . . oh, I forgot . . . you don't like that word. There's this douche bag up here who's giving me trouble."

I would murmur a weak "Oh, Fred" (I felt I should), and he was off on one more long story of boats missed and islands lost and women left wailing on the dock.

He called the office. Galleys were left unread, meetings postponed, secretaries stood waving in the doorway, while I, feet propped on an open desk drawer, listened, laughed, and tried to figure out what on earth he was talking about. He became a local legend, like the editor of my youth who thought her possibly forgotten cigarettes would incinerate us all, and would have her assistant scour her office for an hour after she herself had left for home, looking for insufficiently snuffed-out stubs. "Frederick Exley is on the phone," my secretary would whisper to the supplicants, and my absences were forgiven.

He called me at home, sometimes yanking me out of bed at three in the morning. He had seen an old girlfriend, a twenty-two-year-old with skin like satin and hair like corn-silk and legs like inverted bowling pins. They had had a *contretemps*. Did I understand it?

"Fred," I would answer, "I cannot spend the night dissecting the thought processes of ex-cheerleaders."

The doctor of one of his former wives had made a pass at her. What should he do?

"Nothing," I'd say. "It's not your problem."

His publisher has done this; his agent has done that; and Alfred Kazin is a fuck. "Yes," I say. An admirer of Kazin's, I am lying. But lying is preferable to listening to an exegesis on Alfred Kazin's fuckhood.

Letters arrived, too, a folderful of letters, in one of which he told me that if I wanted to bring my daughters for a holiday to Alex Bay, he would vacate his pad and we could have it for free and we would love it. We would love it because the St. Lawrence River flows through his backyard, there is a cinder-block fireplace on which we can barbecue, as well as a picnic table and benches. I was about to dab my eyes, moved by this middle-American scenario, when I read the next sentence. He had caught yet one more dose of the clap in Florida, but the drip seemed to be drying. I put the handkerchief away and laughed helplessly. Fred was my bouncing baby boy, and I loved him.

To listen to Fred was to go down the rabbit hole. His

world, which was wholly bounded by his skull, was a world in which everything was tilted, and nothing was as it appeared, not even pain. Walk into it, and you looked at your life through windows that had the bubbles and distortions of eighteenth-century glass. I didn't want to see my life plain. Clarity seemed a curse. Too, I was captivated by obscenity, because I never used it myself. (When, in the course of one day, Fred managed to anger his agent, his editor, and me, the agent, a woman, yelled, "Fuck you!" His editor shrieked, "Cocksucker!" I said, "That was damn rude, Fred.")

Fred's language was in Technicolor. My own was in black and white. And he attracted friends for much the same reason a burning building attracts spectators. We were mesmerized by the flames and falling rafters and buckling walls, we who kept our houses under a thin film of ice. But Fred's house was never totally consumed, and I, who was always frozen, had become used to warming my hands at its heat.

When I stepped from the tiny plane in Lanai, he handed me a necklace, a plastic dolphin on a chain — "in lieu of a lei" — grumbled when he heard the airline had lost my luggage ("You would, Cantwell, you would"), led me to the portable bar that was the jeep, introduced me to Jo and Phyllis, and deposited me at the island's one store. The airline had said I could charge up to $25.

There were no nightgowns, so I bought a T-shirt, extra large, that said LANAI '76. Toothpaste, but forgot to ask for a toothbrush. No makeup. They didn't have any. Shampoo. Underpants of a style I had assumed was discontinued around 1958. The bill was $12.76, and Fred and Jo berated me for not having had the wit to expend the remaining $12.24 on a stack of sixpacks.

One doesn't wear shoes in Hawaiian houses, and the floors were chilly, so Fred gave me his socks. The nights are cool, so he gave me his basketball jacket. Walking through the small living room, seeing me ensconced on his couch with a wineglass in my hand and my eyes on a televised basketball game, he shouted, "Fifteen fuckin' minutes in this fuckin' house and you've absconded with my fuckin' whole damn wardrobe."

I think he was glad to see me.

The house was on a dirt road lined with others like it: close together, backyard vegetable gardens, the sounds of cocks crowing and hens clucking and of television sets in every living room. Sometimes, before dinner, I took a walk, afraid to wander too far, because there were no streetlights and night came thick and fast. Even the stars, stars I had never seen so close and dense, couldn't penetrate the darkness.

Imagine us at dinner, at the kitchen table, which we seldom left before bedtime. "Fred," Phyllis says, "tell Mary about the time the telephone company detective came to your house." Fred, tapdance for the lady.

"Well, I was off the booze and out jogging, trying to get some of this fuckin' fat off. I came home and was standing in the kitchen in my little sweatsuit pouring some fuckin' Seven-Up in a fuckin' clean glass when the doorbell rings and this guy in a blue suit and wingtips tells me he's a detective and would like to ask a few questions.

"The FBI was always doing employment checks on my former students, so I let him in and poured him some fuckin Seven-Up in a fuckin' clean glass. I even gave him some fuckin' ice cubes.

"He says, 'We've had some complaints about your making obscene phone calls, Mr. Exley.'

"I was scared shitless. I've done some time on the funny farm, y'know, and I thought, 'Jeezus! I've flipped out again and I don't even know if I've been calling old ladies'" — he crossed his eyes and dangled his tongue — "'and going huh-huh-huh into the phone.' Then I remember my mother's asleep in the next room and she's going to come out, rubbing her eyes, just in time to see her son, Fat Freddie E, being led off in a straitjacket.

"I finally get the balls to say, 'But I haven't been making any obscene phone calls,' and he says, 'But the girls have reported . . .'

"'Wait a minute. Who do you work for?'

"'The telephone company.'"

"'The phone company? You mean the operators . . . _those_ dumb bunnies?' All the time I thought he was the FBI! And here I'd given him my fuckin' Seven-Up. In a fuckin' clean glass. With fuckin' ice cubes! _My_ Seven-Up!

"The way I see it, Cantwell, the operators are there to work. But what the hell do they do? I was trying to call the mainland last week and the operator said" — he lifted his voice a few notes — "'Sir, that number can be dialed direct.' And I said, 'Please, ma'am. I've got this paralyzed right arm and I can't . . .' And she said, 'Sir, that number can be dialed direct.'

"'My left arm is paralyzed, too.' 'Sir, I told you, that number _can be dialed direct_.' 'Lady,' I say, 'the truth is I'm paralyzed from head to foot and I've been sitting here five minutes trying to get an erection so I can dial.'"

Fred's words fly, like ascending columns of birds, up, up, up, until finally they are out the window and into space, where we can't follow them. "Disagree with him, Mary," Phyllis nudges me, as still another diatribe against the armed forces, the entertainment industry, the communications industry, the fuckin' New York literati, takes flight and whizzes past us.

"I can't," I answer. "I never disagree with Fred."

Sometimes, though, I am frightened for him when I realize how slippery is the edge on which he lives. One time I am sad for him, when, in the midst of a harangue about women and the way they drive — they _force_ men to violence — he says, "If only I could love somebody," and I see the terrible roots of misogyny.

Still, he is a lover, even of women, provided he can forget their sex. He is loyal to his buddies and as generous as a fool, and he has arranged for me to stay in the local doctor's guesthouse, where I read all day and dispense beer and dry-roasted peanuts to him and Jo and Phyllis and the doctor and his pregnant wife from four o'clock on. Once I try to provide dinner, but when I go to the island store, I find nothing, but for a pig's head staring at me from the freezer, that I recognize.

"You're Fred's friend from the mainland," the proprietor says. (I must be. There are only eight Caucasians on this island, the eighth being me.) "We have some Chab-liss you could try." So I buy two bottles, along with a Maui onion and some ground beef so that I can do burgers.

"Jeez!" Fred says when everybody arrives. "And you claim to be a cook!"

I wear his dolphin for luck and, although my luggage has shown up, his socks for security. When he mentions the balding man, who he knows was my friend but does not know was my lover, and I start to cry and stop, embarrassed and blaming my tears on overwork and overtiredness and maybe a kind of craziness, he says, "Don't worry, Mary. My views on craziness are a little different from other people's. You're not crazy. Just aim for a selective memory, like mine."

But I will never have a selective memory. Mine is out of

control. It provides me either with everything or with nothing, and is triggered by my senses, which are far keener and far more intractable than my brain.

There is an evening when we are around the kitchen table and I say . . . what, I don't remember now, but it evokes from Jo: "We've got another crazy Irishman on our hands."

"Who's the first?" I ask.

"Fred."

"Fred!" I am surprised, because his surname is as English as, say, Windsor.

"Don't let my last name — I love my last name — fool you. How I've hated being Irish! I'm always trying to disguise it. Phyllis, remember all those clothes I ordered from the Abercrombie and Fitch catalogue? But, Jesus, am I Irish!"

I look at him very hard, past the thick beard and the thatch of gray hair, and see a pair of familiar-seeming, flat brown eyes staring back at me.

"Fred!" I start to laugh. "The beard fooled me. You look like my Uncle Bill. I've run five thousand miles and found my Uncle Bill."

But he was not my Uncle Bill, because my Uncle Bill was not the son of a telephone lineman and a woman who stood behind the steam table in the high school cafeteria. My Uncle Bill didn't have to have a friend pretend that he, not Fred, was So-and-So's date for the prom because the girl's parents wouldn't have wanted her seen with him. My Uncle Bill knew nothing of the rage that had Fred screwing in adulthood the wives of the boys who had snubbed him in childhood. My Uncle Bill was an executive in a rubber company, not an open wound that could be bandaged only with words. All the time Fred had me laughing and gasping and throwing up my hands, I was wondering why a man who was so drunk was also so curiously clearheaded. That he often struck me as mad was another thing entirely.

I was living in the suspended time that follows grief, when the nervous system shuts down and only the heart and lungs and muscles are working, those and the part of the head that permits dailiness. Except for the moment when Fred mentioned the balding man and a nerve jumped and made me cry, I was insulated. The insulation was not willed. Rather, my body had taken over for my brain and was giving it a few weeks' peace.

Thrice I was jolted into happiness. The first night on Lanai, before I could move into the guesthouse, Fred gave me his bedroom — iron bed, creaky bedsprings, shabby deal bureau, typewriter on a table, a varnished bookcase jammed with paperbacks, no curtains — but I couldn't sleep. I was too infatuated with the susurration of banana leaves against the window screens and, at dawn, the roosters' wakeup calls. I was happy, too, on the afternoon I first dispensed beer and peanuts to the group and thought, "What nice people." Both times I was also thinking, "And I got here *all by myself.*"

The third time was the night we had dinner at the young doctor's house and I sat on the floor eating sukiyaki and drinking warm sake. Beside me sat Phyllis's father, a barefoot nut-brown man who spoke only Tagalog. He laughed when I laughed, looked sober when I looked sober, showed his appreciation for the food with deep, rumbling burps, and wound me in the peace that comes when there is no possibility of talk. I was, I am, so tired of talking.

Then the newspaperman arrived.

He had been covering what Fred called the year's major sporting events — the Superbowl, a prizefight in Las Vegas, and Gary Gilmore's execution — and had called from Los

Angeles, sobbing and exhausted. "Come to Lanai," Fred said. "Leave that fuckin' job. Take some fuckin' time off."

"Poor guy," he told Jo, Phyllis, and me, "those fuckin' bastards are squeezing him to death."

I didn't like the newspaperman. Perhaps it is simply that I was prepared to resent anyone who pierced that small circle in which I was seeking deafness and blindness, and turned it into what Fred called Payne Whitney West. Or perhaps it is the malice bred from consciousness of one's self-control that makes me say I wish he had just hung a sign reading I AM A TORTURED PERSON around his neck and let up on the theatrics.

We were in the guesthouse living room when he started telling us about the newsmen near the prison, the television cameras, and, finally, the procession into the execution shed and past the execution chair, led by a tour guide who counted out the five bullet holes. One bullet had been a blank so that the riflemen were all able to participate in one of their fellows' accidental innocence. The newspaperman acted it out, repeated the dialogue, and paced the living room, pretending to be a television announcer, a guard, the tour guide.

It was ironic. I had run as far as I could from memories of the balding man but was reminded of him time and time again by Fred, who spoke often of famous writers he had known or brushed against, because it made him feel a member of their church. And, horrified that murder was legal again, I had run from all the brouhaha that preceded Gilmore's death, because it meant that once more I, who had been told by an uncle in childhood that execution meant that someone set your hair on fire, would once again dream of my head bursting into flames. But both had followed me to Lanai.

How could I not hate the messenger with the bad news?

Execution was in the room, and with it the photographs I remembered blazoned on the front pages of the tabloids on my first few weeks in New York. The Rosenbergs were to die, and I, just out of college, apolitical, and soon to marry a boy who, though almost as apolitical as I, was Jewish and thus possibly scarred with the mark of Cain, was about to be caught and fried for crimes unimagined as well as uncommitted. I wasn't crazy. Truly. It was just that young, missing my father, torn (willingly) from the WASPS and laid-back Catholics who had constituted the bastion that was my childhood, I had traveled too far from home.

Fred slept on the guesthouse couch that night; the newspaperman had his bed in Jo and Phyllis's cottage. Actually, Fred didn't sleep — he seldom slept — and I heard the pop of beer cans opening and the soft padding of his bare feet as he walked between the couch and the television set.

I was frightened. I had toppled off the edge of the world. I kept seeing the last walk, that last mile, and I was the walker. I remembered lying along the balding man's magic back, how he moored me as a piling does a skiff. He had said, "Mah Mary, make me a statement. *Do you love me?*" Was it possible I hadn't answered? Or had I, and spoken too softly? What else had I done wrong? Was it because I went to *Einstein on the Beach* on the night he had said he would arrive in New York since I knew him to be unreliable and *Einstein* was rumored to be unmissable? But he did arrive when promised, and found me, not planted by the phone, as I was supposed to be, but out. Or was it because I hadn't understood that leaving him in an empty bed was like leaving him in a desert?

I wished I could go into the living room and ask Fred to get into bed with me, to be a stuffed animal I could hold until I slept. But I had never asked that of anyone. Besides,

Fred had said once, "I never ball anyone I like," and might have felt compelled to say no. He might have thought I wanted more than a teddy bear.

When the dark faded to gray, I heard the screen door slam. I got up, dressed, and went back to my work, my old companion. I did that almost every day on Lanai, sitting at a card table with notes and a pile of typing paper. I was sifting through memories — of the way snow hitting the hot air at the bottom of the air shaft outside our first apartment bounced up again, say, and of B rubbing my back when I was in labor with Snow White — thinking that if I wrote them down, they would form a shape, make sense. I was looking for cause and effect, not knowing then that often there are no links, only happenstance.

At five o'clock every day Fred would arrive in the jeep to fetch me for dinner, restless and anxious to get back to Jo and Phyllis and the kitchen table, where he was safe. I was a nuisance but a diversion, too, and once when Jo said, "Mary, why don't you move to one of the bigger islands — you can do your editing from there — and take this old goat with you?" I saw a little flicker in Fred's dead eyes. The promise of normality, of a well-regulated life, always lured him, though only for a second.

With the newspaperman's arrival the balance of power had shifted. We were no longer four friends at a kitchen table, but three boys sitting in a tarpaper clubhouse and two girls they wouldn't let in the door. Not that their conversation fascinated Phyllis and me. I doubt it fascinated them.

"What kind of an expense account you got? . . . Yeah? Must be rough out there on the road . . . Yeah? Must be a lot of boozin' . . . Suppose you have to bury the liquor bills somewhere, huh? . . . Yeah? The fucks!"

Sometimes Jo looked down the table at Phyllis and me. I

could tell he wanted to hear what we were saying, maybe even join us, but that would have meant breaking a club rule, so he didn't.

Fred had taken a walk alone every night before dinner, but no more. After he'd been gone for ten minutes, the newspaperman would say, "Guess I'll go look for Fred," and go out, to reappear with him about half an hour later. He was like a sheepdog working a flock, only he was working Fred out, not in. Perhaps if the newspaperman's wife had been there we would have achieved détente. The girls could have done the dishes while the boys talked. Alone with Phyllis and me, the newspaperman never spoke. I guess he felt we had no common denominator.

I take that back. Once he spoke to me. We were in the back of Jo's jeep, and he said, "I read your article about Fred. Enjoyed it."

"Thank you. I'd like to read the one you did on him for ———," and I named his newspaper.

We turned and looked at our mutual subject, the Pulitzer Prize nominee. He was standing twenty feet away, legs spraddled, urinating against a tree. The newspaperman's face was expressionless. I was trying not to laugh.

Later, returned to New York, I embroidered a dinner party with my anger at the newspaperman — how, working out his formidable *angst*, he, equipped with a snorkel, had made a Byronic run toward the Pacific and settled instead for a racing dive into a tide pool; how, gypping me of my longed-for place in the fishing boat, he had set out to snare a marlin while stoked on Dramamine.

"Maybe you felt you were half of a couple before he arrived," a friend said.

I thought about that statement. I think about what anyone says of me with the concentration of a watch repairer looking for a faulty cog. No, she wasn't right. I was angry because the newspaperman had pushed me into the cold. He was an intruder who hogged the fire around which we were all keeping warm. I was jealous, too, because he and Fred excluded me, jealous the way Jo was the night he ordered Phyllis to bed because he found the two of us speaking low. I think we were talking about children. It didn't matter. Jo thought we were telling our secrets, and maybe, in a sense, we were.

But the anger evaporated; my anger always does, because I am distracted by small pleasures, as easily charmed as a cranky baby responding to a well-placed tickle. One afternoon Phyllis and I walked along the little beach and across the black rocks to a cliff, down which we climbed to a semicircle of sand called Shark Cove. We didn't have much in common besides life, I supppose, but sometimes that can be enough. While we waded, the waves curling like cream around our footprints, I told her about the balding man, and Phyllis told me about her first husband and a lover she once had. We scaled the cliff to rejoin the gentlemen and never spoke of those men again. Strangers on a train we were, getting off at our different stops with a little less luggage than when we had boarded.

I don't know how long I was on Lanai — a week or ten days, maybe — but it was long enough to slip into its spin. I loved shopping in the one store and trying to construct fettucini Alfredo out of Japanese noodles and processed cheese, and most of all I liked nodding to people who were beginning to recognize me as I trundled down the aisles with my cart. When the young doctor's wife came back from one of the big islands with her sonograms, she shared the photographs of the little blob in her uterus with Phyllis and me. Was it a boy? A girl? I often wonder. Did the rich American woman, an anomaly on Lanai, ever get her longed-for hot tub? Are Jo and Phyllis still there? Are the roads still rutted? Is dawn still a matter of crows and hens and the stirrings of banana leaves? Never mind. It will be until my brain shuts down.

My last night on Lanai the newspaperman, dizzied by alcohol and Dramamine, passed out in Fred's room. Jo, drunk, had gone to bed. Fred had fallen asleep on the living room couch. There was no one to drive the jeep through the dark to the little guesthouse, so Phyllis pulled an air mattress onto the living room floor and gave me a muumuu, which, since she had an Asian's small bones, I shimmied into like a snake retrieving a shed skin.

Then she, too, went to bed, and I lay on the floor thinking about returning to the mainland — there was no choice nor did I really want one, because all islands are, in the end, too small — and listening to a cacophony of snores.

Fred's I could endure — they were deep and rhythmic — but the newspaperman gurgled between snorts. I crawled across the room on my hands and knees, V'd my index and middle fingers around the knob, and slowly pulled his door shut.

I was making my way back to the air mattress when I suddenly thought of the sight I must make: sausaged into a muumuu and creeping. I looked around at this latest place to which my feet had brought me. To my left, a small, feisty man and his Filipino wife were snoring in their bedroom. Behind me, the tortured newspaperman was snoring in Fred's bedroom. To my right was Fred himself, snoring on the couch.

I was, at that moment, literally on my knees. But I was moving. I was laughing, too. "Mary," I said to this woman I had lived with so long, "I've enjoyed knowing you."

Nine

Not long ago I was standing on the corner of Second Avenue and Fourteenth Street, waiting for a crosstown bus, when the smell of some kind of spicy food curled, almost like a veil, around my nose. It came from one of the nearby restaurants, though I knew neither which one nor which country's cuisine was on its menu. But I had been in that country, I knew, because the aroma brought me back to twilight and the end of a day's sightseeing and narrow streets thronged with people on their way home. It was always, I remember, "the hour between the dog and the wolf," the hour in which I, no matter how pleasant the circumstances, longed for a roof between me and the sky. And for a few minutes, sniffing that spicy scent — a kind of curry, it may have been — I knew again the loneliness I had known so well.

But it was my neighborhood in which I was waiting, my bus I was soon to board, my people, however different their blood and their pasts were from mine, with whom I was sharing complaints about five o'clock traffic and buses in happy herds camping out by the East River. I was going home to my place and my table. I would shut the door on the dark and sink into a cave of my own making. That's what all houses are really, caves. Of course one reads about houses with big windows and big sliding doors, those houses designed to "bring nature indoors." But how much do you want to bet that, once the sun goes down, the blinds will be drawn and the curtains closed on those monuments to glass and T-beams? It is pleasant to lie in bed, as I do, with the shutters parted and the moon riding between them. But to sit in a curtainless living room and feel the night pressing in is to realize that the dark can be much stronger than bricks and mortar. Better not to look.

The bus, finally separated from its herd, arrived, and I got on to sit next to the window, because I can never get enough of looking at New York City. No matter how often I travel crosstown, for instance, the people are people I have never seen before, the building that was naked on Tuesday is tracked with scaffolding and swathed in orange netting on Thursday. An old sign is scarcely down before a new sign goes up. The seafood place is now a tapas bar, the second-hand bookstore is suddenly a health food emporium. The notion that there are bucks to be made, if one can only find the right angle, the right goods, never goes out of style in New York.

Getting off at Ninth Avenue, I took a short cut to my apartment, past the impossibly long-legged transvestite hookers, who, after the occasional police sweep, invariably migrate back to the meat market district. Because it was chilly, a few fires had already been started in the rusted metal barrels, and I started one myself, in my fireplace, when I got home. Of all the cities in the world, New York is the most sensual. No mangoes or papayas grow here, and oranges are not for stripping from the trees. Summer breezes are humid and laced with the stink of asphalt, low tide, and, if you're near a subway entrance or a boarded vacant lot, urine. But my senses are enlivened here as they are nowhere else in the world.

The sensuality emerges from disparity. There is a vast distance between the fire in the fireplace and the one in the trash barrel, a million miles between the "ching-ching-chong" (or so it sounds to me) of Chinatown mothers chattering to the babies strapped to their chests and the subdued purr of Upper East Side nannies pushing baby buggies as big and as soundless as Rolls-Royces. A stretch limo, analogous to the motor car in _Mrs. Dalloway,_ in which passersby had "just time to see a face of the very greatest importance against the dove-gray upholstery," slips down Fifth Avenue. This time, too, mystery — who is it? could it have been . . . ? — brushes the passersby with her wing. One block west, on Sixth Avenue, a woman naked from the waist up sprawls in a doorway, picking lice off her breasts.

"I've got to get away," I say to myself when I see that part of the city and its life, which make me want to curl into a creature as blind and deaf and unfeeling as an earthworm. "I've _got_ to get away." But when I watch the sun dropping into the Hudson like a polished penny slipping through a slot, or a neighbor stubbornly planting pansies at the foot of a street tree, I am turned into Lot's wife. The pansies won't last; nothing lasts here. But nothing ever changes either. There will always be the sun setting into the Hudson and a New Yorker fighting cement with pansies, and as long as I am able, I will be trying desperately to take it all in. "Your eyes are too big for your belly," my grandmother warned me over and over again. I heard her and remember the warning, but what should I do? Shut them to the pleasures and torments of this place? They are, after all, what drew me here. What keeps me here, too.

I don't travel now, at least not the way I used to, although

I still talk, albeit more casually these days, to strangers. But before I left the magazine for a newspaper at which I sat day after day making endless phone calls, asking endless questions, and drawing endless conclusions (the job was, I used to tell friends, rather like being a brain on a plate), I went on a few press junkets. One was to France, to celebrate Perrier, but once in Paris I hardly ever left my room at the Crillon because I couldn't bear to part with walls covered with apricot-colored silk and a tub encased in mahogany. Another time I was in France again, but in the Cognac region. I don't remember much about it except that the weather was cold and the trees skeletal, and I ate three different fresh foie gras, each slab brandishing a little flag. The best junket was to Spain, where, the ticket having an open return, I eventually stayed with friends on the Costa del Sol. But first I had to endure a week of education about the growing, harvesting, and packing of olives. Part of the procedure involved someone's standing for hours on a wooden block, scraping seeds off pimientos. Another took sitting at what looked like an old-fashioned school desk and crooking one's arm over a little jar so as to, with tongs, arrange the olives in pretty tiers. Whenever, rarely, I drink a martini, I am reminded of torture. "If you only knew," I am half-disposed to say to my fellow drinkers, "what went into getting that stuffed olive into your glass!" Then I console myself by thinking (I have, despite considerable evidence to the contrary, great faith in the mind of man) that there must now be a technological solution to seeding pimientos and inserting olives into jars.

I loved those junkets, the camaraderie imposed by drowsy day trips to Source Perrier and barrel-making factories and olive fields, and, in the evening, the afterdinner giggles over which unattached male company executive was after which pretty young editor. Actually, the males were never unattached, but their wives, out of sight, were also out of mind.

I loved the sharing of eyeshadow and tips about lip liner, and the way one or another of us was always called upon to order the teeth on the inevitable spine-tracking zipper on somebody's long evening dress. All the junkets ended in elaborate dinner parties, and even though we knew the speeches would be boring and the entertainment second-rate, we were as enveloped in bath powder and perfume and expectation as if this night was prom night. After a certain age — thirty-five seems about right — one cannot count on ever again knowing the girlishness that comes of a flirtation. But feeling silk against your skin or the way your hair is falling — _just right_ — along your cheek never fails.

Now I go to Australia, the country I assumed I would never see again.

Snow White and Rose Red had inherited a little money. The latter, predictably, spent hers on graduate school. The former, also predictably, headed straight to Newark Airport, where she waited three days for a flight to London on an airline whose finances were so precarious that it never took off until all the seats were sold.

Once in a while I would lose track of her, but never for long, because she often made midnight calls from pay phones in the middle of nowhere. When, as was frequent, she ran out of change, she would hurriedly give me the number and I'd ring back. Sometimes I didn't know which European city I was dialing. But she was well, she was happy, and if I have never received precise descriptions of the towns in which she stayed and the streets along which she walked, it is not because she didn't want to tell me. It is because Snow White is such an assiduous keeper of journals that all her words go into them. Little is real to her unless she writes it down. If I were to ask her, for instance, what hiking through the Scottish Highlands is like, she would have to consult one of her journals to find out.

Then one day she came home with a young Australian met in a Dublin bus station (their hands touched as they reached for the same street map), and suddenly I had a son. He had red hair and blue eyes and a gap between his two front teeth, and when I baked bread he pulled a rocker into the kitchen to keep me company. When he wanted Snow White to go to Brisbane with him (he was bent on marriage), I said, "Go, because Australia is a wonderful country and, besides, his kind doesn't come twice."

So she went, but less because of him perhaps than because of Lillian. "She's still taking care of me," she said.

The marriage did not last, but Australia did, and Snow White is there, in Sydney, in a little house furnished mostly with furniture she has found on the street and with my mother's needlepoint pillows. My mother also paints tole trays and little boxes and sends them to her, along with watercolors of Bristol scenes she bought years ago from Bristol's old Women's Exchange. The Women's Exchange, which took consignments only from the certifiably genteel, is where a lot of Bristol matrons bought wedding presents when I was a child. It is strange. Just as I found a semblance of my Uncle Bill on Lanai, so I have found a semblance of Bristol on a continent thirteen thousand miles away. I see my mother with her needle, her canvas, and her skeins of yarn. I see her sitting at a kitchen table, which has been spread with newspapers, drawing a gold line on a black enamel tray with a brush as thin as a hair. When I look at the watercolors, I see Bristol Harbor as it was when I was young, before a factory was built on its south shore and spoiled the vista. I see a dimly recalled gazebo built on a small spit of land not far from our house. I see what Snow White has never seen but what, because she assures me she is psychic ("Lillian came to me the night she died and sat in the rocking chair in my bedroom, and said she would never leave me"), I am convinced she sees anyway.

In Australia I have also found a semblance of myself. It is in my elder daughter. Some children are the spit-and-image of their parents, but usually they are people we have never seen before. It takes only a minute or two to figure that out. But it may take years before we realize that sometimes our children are people unlike any we have ever known. For most of her life I searched for bits and pieces of myself in Snow White, thinking that if I found them we could connect, that we would be like two strips of Velcro finally uniting. But I never found any until she moved to Australia, and then I discovered that my child and I shared the same itchy feet, the same curiosity, the same willingness to wake every morning to a new vista. "You are," she told me a year or so ago, "my favorite traveling companion." Sleeping over pubs because we cannot find a hotel room, taking buses whose destinations we don't quite know, feeding loaves of bread to kangaroos, shivering at the terror that is a Tasmanian Devil and at the glory that is a cockatoo — we are, while in transit, one person.

Recently we were wandering through an amusement park in Melbourne, built in the 1930s and entered through a huge, laughing mouth. Around the perimeter was a roller coaster, its dips so gentle we thought it worth daring (neither of us looks for things that might frighten us, because we know too well that they are looking for us). But when we went up to the booth for tickets, we were told the roller coaster was temporarily out of order.

How I had wanted that ride on the roller coaster, not so

much for the journey itself but because it would, in a sense, bring us full circle! Here we would be, my baby and I, side by side again and, as in the years when her life was bounded by a room with bunny wallpaper, a rundown park with rubber swings, and a mother who, whatever her faults, was always good for a bedtime story, looking in the same direction.

My disappointment was erased the next morning, though, when Snow White came to my hotel to pick me up for the ride to the airport. It was very early, so I was sitting in bed sipping coffee and reading the newspaper. She slid in next to me, picked up the section I had finished, and, the paper still in her hand, dozed off, with her head resting on my shoulder.

When she was born I cried, because until that moment I hadn't realized that in giving her life I was also giving her death. I wanted her back in my womb so that I could keep her safe and warm for as long as I lived. Now, her sleeping head against my shoulder, she was safe and warm again, and once more I was pregnant with my first-born.

It is easy to write about sorrow dry-eyed, but not about joy. When I remember that morning in Melbourne, my eyes get wet, but no more so than they do when I am watching Fred Astaire dancing. It is happiness that makes me cry, happiness and maybe some kind of as yet undiscovered gene that's handed down from Celt to Celt and sometimes makes weepers of us all. "Ah, Mary Lee," my father said when I was sobbing over my introduction to "Sailing to Byzantium," "you're a sentimental Irishman, just like your old man." Ah, Papa, you were right.

Rose Red I have met before, mostly in my grandmother. At her christening she was given my grandmother's name and, with it, her tenacity and self-discipline and impatience with what Rose Red calls the "artsy-fartsy" and what Ganny

called "nonsense." In my childhood, Ganny cured my occasional sadness by taking me to play bingo and tour our town's
five-and-ten. In my adulthood, Rose Red does it by dragging
me to Bloomingdale's and Saks Fifth Avenue. "I think my
mother could use a brighter blush," she says to the woman at
the cosmetics counter, and I extend a docile cheek.

She loves books and movies, but, unlike me, she does not
look to them for wisdom, only amusement. For instruction
she goes directly to life itself, and it is life that she is forever
steering me toward. There is something of my father in her,
too. Like him, she expects a lot from me, courage mostly, and
if I have ever been brave it is because she has forced me to
be. Knowing her, I now believe that the greatest favor one
can do people is to ask of them more than they think they
can give.

The day she married I thought to find her nervous,
frightened even, as I was on my wedding day. But the only
nervous person walking down the aisle was I, coupled once
more with her father. She had a swan's serenity. I, while we
delivered her to her fiancé and the judge who performed the
ceremony, was fighting tears until I sat down and reached for
Snow White's hand.

Still, despite all that Rose Red has done to show me what
matters and what does not, I remain confused. My head is so
crowded with long-ago images and concluded conversations
that I cannot shut the lid on myself. Some people marvel at
my memory; others, novelists usually, distrust my ilk. They
believe that those of us who write memoirs are, in truth,
writing fiction. "How," they ask, "can these people _remem-
ber_ so much?" But we can. In fact, we cannot always see the
present until it is the past, which means that, although some
part of our brain is observing and preserving the moment,
we are not truly living it. Years later, though, it will be

resurrected, more often than not without our willing it. "I write," I've told those who've cared to inquire, "because I have mud between my ears, and writing is my way of making things clear." But the statement is inaccurate. It is not mud but a logjam that is between my ears.

Twice the logjam exploded and set my mind to moving as smoothly as a river. The first time was when I had Rocky Mountain spotted fever and thought I might die. The second time was recently when, again, I thought I might die. My response to both scares was the same. "My duty was done," I have written of the fever, "and the last thing I would see with earth's eyes was my daughters, my descendants, growing like trees."

Even so, something was different about the second terror. There was no balding man to wonder whether or not to call. He was dead. Nor, although I would have liked to speak to him, did I think of calling B. He has always been very much on my mind, but I suspect I disappeared from his many years ago. What could we have possibly said to each other? Unlike those people with whom I had laughed and chatted and, yes, communed while I was roaming around the world, he was not a stranger. Ergo, communication, above all communion, was impossible. We knew each other too well.

Instead, I turned off the ringer on my phone, was cheerful for the sake of the few people I had told about my illness, and spent most of the time, day and night, staring out my hospital window. The room was high up, on the fourteenth floor, I think, and all I saw was a sky into which intruded the spires of several buildings and the occasional small plane. There were books I could have read and magazines scattered at the foot of my bed, but morphine had me slightly dozy, the way I am just before I settle down for sleep. So I drew out the long gray ribbon, the one with the brightly colored

blocks with which I so often amuse myself. One of the
blocks, one I had not examined for many years, was of the
day soon after college graduation when I emerged from a
train into Grand Central Terminal, a leather-cased Smith
Corona portable in one hand and a suitcaseful of unsuitable
— old Bermuda shorts, Brooks Brothers shirts, a gingham
skirt, and a dress for after-football cocktail parties — clothes
in the other. That was the day, I realized on the instant, that
I embraced my true bridegroom. That was the day I married
New York.